THE CLAUSAL THEORY OF TYPES

Cambridge Tracts in Theoretical Computer Science

Titles in the series

THE CLAUSAL THEORY OF TYPES

D.A. WOLFRAM
University of Oxford

CAMBRIDGE
UNIVERSITY PRESS

CAMBRIDGE UNIVERSITY PRESS
Cambridge, New York, Melbourne, Madrid, Cape Town, Singapore, São Paulo, Delhi

Cambridge University Press
The Edinburgh Building, Cambridge CB2 8RU, UK

Published in the United States of America by Cambridge University Press, New York

www.cambridge.org
Information on this title: www.cambridge.org/9780521117906

First published 1993
This digitally printed version 2009

A catalogue record for this publication is available from the British Library

ISBN 978-0-521-39538-0 hardback
ISBN 978-0-521-11790-6 paperback

Contents

Preface

The development of first-order logic programming can be traced back to resolution theorem proving and further to the Skolem-Herbrand-Gödel Theorem, a fundamental theorem of first-order logic. This book proceeds by providing an extrapolation of this development to a higher-order setting. More precisely, it presents a largely theoretical foundation of a form of higher-order resolution, and combined functional and logic programming.

The Clausal Theory of Types is a higher-order logic for which the Skolem-Herbrand--Gödel Theorem and resolution can be generalized. It is a clausal extensional sub-logic of Church's formulation of the Simple Theory of Types which includes equality. It is "higher--order" in the sense that it allows quantification of variables of all types, embeddable predicates, representations of functions and predicates by λ-abstractions, and equations involving abstractions.

All of these features enable its Horn clause form to be a concise logic and functional programming language which has a sound and complete declarative and operational semantics. Clausal Theory of Types logic programs incorporate higher-order functional evaluation as an elementary operation through unification or conditional higher-order rewriting, higher-order relational proofs through backtrack search, and the separation of their declarative specifications.

This extrapolation entails largely self-contained discussions on the development of resolution and logic programming, the simply typed λ-calculus, higher-order logics and Henkin-Andrews general models, higher-order forms of term rewriting and equational unification, and higher-order versions of the Resolution Theorem and fixed point, model theoretic, and operational results in logic programming. There is also a survey of results on higher-order unification, and approaches to solving whether higher-order matching is decidable.

Acknowledgements

I thank David Tranah and Roger Astley of Cambridge University Press, and Keith van Rijsbergen for their assistance in the preparation of this work. I am grateful to: Lawrence Paulson, Thièrry Coquand, Michael Gordon, Roger Hindley, Gérard Huet, Fairouz Kamareddine, Dale Miller, John Mitchell, Paliath Narendran, Philippe Nöel, Arthur Norman, Frank Pfenning, Andrew Pitts, John Shepherdson, and Richard Statman for discussions or comments which were directly related to this work. Sections of the book are based on talks I gave at l'Institut National de Recherche en Informatique et en Automatique (INRIA), Rocquencourt, France in January 1990, University of Cambridge Computer Laboratory in February and November 1990, the Fourth International Conference on Rewriting Techniques and Applications at Como, Italy in April 1991, and the Sixth International Workshop on Unification at Schloß Dagstuhl, Germany in July 1992. Comments by the participants at these meetings and students at lectures on the Clausal Theory of Types led to my changing the presentation of parts of the book.

This work was supported by: Cambridge Philosophical Society; a Junior Research Fellowship at Christ Church, Oxford; Oxford University Computing Laboratory, Programming Research Group; Rae & Edith Bennett Travelling Scholarship; Trinity College, Cambridge; and University of Cambridge Computer Laboratory.

D.A.W.

Oxford
December 1992

Chapter 1

Logic Programming: A Case Study

A semantics of logic programming can be derived from the Skolem-Herbrand-Gödel Theorem of the first-order predicate calculus.

We trace the developments which led to logic programming from automations of theorem proving which used this fundamental result, especially those based on the resolution principle. We also discuss some criteria by which logic programming can be considered to be a programming language, and some of its limitations.

This case study motivates our approach to higher-order logic programming: a higher-order Skolem-Herbrand-Gödel Theorem would give a basis for a more expressive logic programming language.

1.1 From Theorem Provers to Logic Programming

A main task of automated theorem provers is to find whether or not a formula A_{n+1} is a logical consequence of a conjunction of formulas $A_1 \wedge \cdots \wedge A_n$. For first-order classical logic [28], this is a recursively undecidable problem in general [25, 26], however there are semi-decision procedures for testing the validity of a formula which will halt if the formula being tested is valid, but may not halt if the formula is not valid.

Automated theorem provers have been used to answer questions such as "Does there exist a finite semigroup which simultaneously admits a non-trivial antiautomorphism without admitting a non-trivial involution?" [202], to prove Cantor's Theorem [9] and others in set theory, and to verify the correctness of a microprocessor [33].

1.1.1 The Skolem-Herbrand-Gödel Theorem

A fundamental result used in some of these procedures is the Skolem-Herbrand-Gödel Theorem [125][1].

We use the semantics of classical first-order logic [7] in the following discussion. The Skolem-Herbrand-Gödel Theorem concerns the validity of first-order formulas:

Theorem 1.1 *(Skolem-Herbrand-Gödel.) A formula A is valid if and only if a compound instance of a Skolem normal form of $\neg A$ is unsatisfiable.*

---

[1]See the papers by Skolem, Herbrand, and Gödel [84]. The Theorem is also called the Expansion Theorem, or incorrectly referred to as Herbrand's Theorem [88] which is a result in proof theory [49, 71].

1

The Skolem-Herbrand-Gödel Theorem depends on four other theorems. By the deduction theorem for classical first-order predicate calculus, showing

$$A_1 \wedge \cdots \wedge A_n \models A_{n+1}$$

is equivalent to showing

$$\models A_1 \wedge \cdots \wedge A_n \supset A_{n+1}.$$

We need only consider the validity of a formula, rather than showing that it is a logical consequence.

There is also no loss of generality if we only consider the unsatisfiability of a formula in Skolem normal form. This is a consequence of a theorem due to Skolem [63, 179] which states that for every first-order formula F there is a first-order formula F' in Skolem normal form such that

- F' is satisfiable if and only if F is satisfiable.

- F' can be effectively computed from F.

It follows that a formula is valid if and only if the Skolem normal form of its negation is unsatisfiable. The algorithm for transforming a formula to one in Skolem normal form is discussed in Section 1.1.2.

The significance of Skolem normal form depends on the following result [63, 121].

Theorem 1.2 *A formula in Skolem normal form has a model if and only if it has a Herbrand model.*

Herbrand models are also called free models [121] and term models. It follows that an arbitrary first-order formula is valid if and only if the Skolem normal form of its negation has no Herbrand model. The class of Herbrand models is smaller than the class of arbitrary first-order models because they are defined using the constant symbols which only occur in the Skolem normal form of a formula, and possibly one additional individual constant symbol.

This reduction makes automating testing validity possible since the absence of a Herbrand model can be tested by finding whether the Herbrand expansion of a formula in Skolem normal form is unsatisfiable. Herbrand expansions are discussed in Section 1.1.3.

The fourth necessary result to do this is the compactness theorem of propositional logic which ensures that the Herbrand expansion of a Skolem normal form formula is unsatisfiable if and only if one of its compound instances is unsatisfiable. Such compound instances can be recursively enumerated.

Major forms of automated theorem proving in first-order logic such as resolution [124], matings [6], and the connection graph method [8, 17] are based on the Skolem-Herbrand--Gödel Theorem and refinements of it which do not require the negation of a formula to be converted to a normal form. We now present resolution theorem proving as an example, before considering how it has been used in logic programming.

1.1.2 Skolem Normal Form

A formula in Skolem normal form has the form

$$\forall x_1 \cdots \forall x_n \, (C_1 \wedge \cdots \wedge C_m)$$

where the C_i are finite disjunctions of literals for $1 \leq i \leq m$, and $x_1, \ldots, x_n$ are the free variables in $C_1, \ldots, C_m$.

We shall convert the following formula F to its Skolem normal form F'.

$$\neg \exists x \forall y \forall z \neg [(\neg q(x,y) \equiv \exists t[\neg \forall y(q(x,y) \supset \neg p(f(v)))])] \wedge \forall x \neg q(v,x)]$$

Firstly, we take the existential closure of F, eliminate redundant quantifiers, and rename quantified variables so that they are distinct. We obtain:

$$\exists v \neg \exists x \forall y \neg [(\neg q(x,y) \equiv [\neg \forall z(q(x,z) \supset \neg p(f(v)))]) \wedge \forall w \neg q(v,w)]$$

We then eliminate logical constants other than $\neg, \wedge, \vee, \exists$ and $\forall$, and move negations all the way inwards to obtain:

$$\exists v \forall x \exists y [[q(x,y) \vee [\exists z(q(x,z) \wedge p(f(v)))]] \wedge$$
$$[\neg q(x,y) \vee [\forall z(\neg q(x,z) \vee \neg p(f(v)))]] \wedge \forall w \neg q(v,w)]$$

We then move quantifiers to the right, and eliminate $\exists$ by the introduction of Skolem constants. This gives:

$$\forall x[[q(x,g(x)) \vee [q(x,h(x)) \wedge p(f(a))]] \wedge$$
$$[\neg q(x,g(x)) \vee [\forall z(\neg q(x,z) \vee \neg p(f(a)))]] \wedge \forall w \neg q(a,w)]$$

Finally, we move $\forall$ to the left, distribute $\wedge$ over $\vee$, and simplify by deleting any tautologous conjuncts and repeated literals in conjuncts to obtain F':

$$F' \;=\; \forall x \forall z \forall w[[q(x,g(x)) \vee q(x,h(x))] \wedge [q(x,g(x)) \vee p(f(a))] \wedge$$
$$[\neg q(x,g(x)) \vee \neg q(x,z) \vee \neg p(f(a))] \wedge [\neg q(a,w)]]$$

The main steps in forming F' from F are the elimination of logical constants other than $\wedge, \vee$ and $\neg$, the elimination of existential quantifiers by the introduction of Skolem functions, and conversion of a subformula to conjunctive normal form. The process of removing quantifiers by introducing terms containing new function symbols is sometimes called Skolemization. Skolem functions are also called Herbrand-Skolem functions because of the extensive use made of them by Herbrand [88].

1.1.3 Compound Instances

The set of function symbols $\{a, f, g, h\}$ each of which occurs in the formula F' is a signature of function symbols. If such a signature does not contain a constant symbol such as a, one can be added. From this signature, a set of ground terms can be recursively enumerated. It includes the terms

$$a, f(a), g(a), h(a), f(f(a)), f(g(a)), f(h(a)), \ldots$$

This set of ground terms is called the Herbrand Universe of F'.

A Herbrand expansion of a formula in Skolem normal form is an infinite conjunction of Herbrand instances, each of which is formed by replacing every occurrence of a universally quantified variable by a term in the Herbrand Universe, and by deleting its universal quantifier.

Ground positive literals in a Herbrand expansion can be regarded as atomic propositions, and negative literals as negated atomic propositions. A finite conjunction of Herbrand instances of a formula is called a compound instance of the formula. For example,

$$[[q(a, g(a)) \lor q(a, h(a))] \land [q(a, g(a)) \lor p(f(a))] \land$$
$$[\neg q(a, g(a)) \lor \neg q(a, h(f(a))) \lor \neg p(f(a))] \land [\neg q(a, h(a))]] \land$$
$$[[q(f(a), g(f(a))) \lor q(f(a), h(f(a)))] \land [q(f(a), g(f(a))) \lor p(f(a))] \land$$
$$[\neg q(f(a), g(f(a))) \lor \neg q(f(a), g(h(a))) \lor \neg p(f(a))] \land [\neg q(a, h(h(a)))]]]$$

is a compound instance of F'.

By the Compactness Theorem for propositional logic, the Herbrand expansion of a formula is unsatisfiable if and only if there is a compound instance of the formula which is unsatisfiable.

It is decidable whether a compound instance is unsatisfiable; a truth table can be constructed. Moreover the set of compound instances is recursively enumerable.

1.1.4   Testing Validity

By the deduction theorem a formula A_{n+1} is a logical consequence of hypotheses $A_1 \land \cdots \land A_n$ if and only if $A_1 \land \cdots \land A_n \land \neg A_{n+1}$ is unsatisfiable. This suggests the following procedure for testing whether A_{n+1} is a logical consequence of the hypotheses.

1. Form a Skolem normal form F' of $A_1 \land \cdots \land A_n \land \neg A_{n+1}$.

2. Repeatedly generate the next compound instance of F' and test if it is unsatisfiable. If so, halt with the answer 'valid'.

Since validity is recursively undecidable, this is a partial decision procedure which may never terminate if the Herbrand expansion of F' is satisfiable. If it halts, the Herbrand expansion of F' is unsatisfiable and A_{n+1} is a logical consequence of $A_1 \land \cdots \land A_n$.

Apart from its applications to automated theorem proving, as an indication of its generality we now state three major results of classical first-order predicate calculus which are direct consequences of the Skolem-Herbrand-Gödel Theorem [121].

Theorem 1.3 *The set of valid formulas and the set of unsatisfiable formulas of first-order predicate calculus are recursively enumerable.*

Proof: It suffices just to consider the case of valid formulas because a formula is valid if and only if its negation is unsatisfiable. The preceding procedure is suitable for testing validity. □

The next theorem is a special form of the Löwenheim-Skolem Theorem [178].

Theorem 1.4 *Every countably infinite set of formulas which has a model, has a model whose domain of individuals is countable.*

Proof: We can assume without loss of generality that the Skolem normal forms of the negations of the formulas have no constant symbols in common. There are countably many such constant symbols. The Herbrand expansion of each of the formulas must be satisfiable and any truth assignment which verifies all of the expansions immediately gives a countable Herbrand model. □

The third major consequence is the compactness theorem of first-order predicate calculus.

Theorem 1.5 *A countably infinite set of formulas has a model if and only if every finite subset of it has a model.*

In addition, apart from these direct consequences, the Theorem and the corrected version of Herbrand's Theorem [49, 88] imply Gödel's Completeness Theorem of first--order predicate calculus [72].

1.1.5 Unsatisfiability Procedures

For automated theorem proving to be practicable, it must be efficient. Systematically generating compound instances and testing their unsatisfiability is an obvious inefficiency in the previous procedure. Unsatisfiability procedures have been developed to reduce this inefficiency.

Formulas in Skolem normal form can be abbreviated to a form called clause form, which is simpler. This is done by replacing a disjunction of literals by a set containing the literals in the disjunction, by replacing a conjunction of such sets by a set containing the sets in the conjunction, and by removing all universal quantifiers. The set is called a formula, and its elements are called clauses. Renaming variables depends on the identity

$$\forall x_1 \cdots \forall x_n (C_1 \wedge C_2) \equiv (\forall x_1 \cdots \forall x_n C_1) \wedge (\forall x_1 \cdots \forall x_n C_2).$$

A clause is an empty clause, written □, if it is the empty set. A clause form formula is unsatisfiable if it includes the empty clause. A clause form formula which is the empty set is always satisfiable.

For example, the previous formula F' has the clause form:

$$\{\{q(x, g(x)), q(x, h(x))\}, \{q(x, g(x)), p(f(a))\},$$
$$\{\neg q(x, g(x)), \neg q(x, z), \neg p(f(a))\}, \{\neg q(a, w)\}\}$$

Davis and Putnam's method [42] for testing the unsatisfiability of a compound instance works directly with ground clauses; the abbreviated counterpart of compound instances. It is a direct implementation of the procedure above based on the Skolem-Herbrand-Gödel Theorem, and it is very inefficient. Attempts by Prawitz [160] and Davis [43] to improve its efficiency led to the resolution method of Robinson [166].

In its ground form, resolution extends one of the three rules of Davis and Putnam's method; the one-literal rule. The rule states that a formula is unsatisfiable if it includes two singleton clauses $\{P\}$ and $\{\neg P\}$. Ground resolution can be seen as a generalization of this rule and a form of Gentzen's cut rule [70] or generalized *modus ponens*. It uses a single rule of inference which is called the ground resolution principle:

> *Choose any two clauses C_1 and C_2 in a set of ground clauses one of which contains a literal P and the other which contains a literal $\neg P$. Include the resolvent clause $C_1 \cup C_2 - \{P, \neg P\}$ in the set of clauses.*

The clause $C_1 \cup C_2 - \{P, \neg P\}$ is called the ground resolvent of the chosen clauses. The initial set of ground clauses is unsatisfiable if and only if after a finite number of applications of the ground resolution principle, the empty clause is a resolvent. The process of forming ground resolvents always terminates with a set which either contains the empty clause, or which contains all possible resolvents. Although ground resolution only uses one rule of inference, it is still impractical for theorem proving based on the Skolem-Herbrand-Gödel Theorem.

Ground resolution depends on checking that complementary ground literals in clauses match. In a similar way, general resolution depends on ensuring that complementary literals in two clauses can be unified. It is more efficient than ground resolution because unification makes forming ground clauses unnecessary.

Unification finds a most general unifier of sets of pairs of literals. The instance of the literals by their most general unifier is their most common general instance: every matching ground instance of two literals is an instance of it. An algorithm using transformations similar to those for first-order unification appears in Herbrand's thesis [88]. Another unification algorithm was given by Robinson [166], who showed that unifiability is decidable and that there always exists a most general unifier of sets of pairs of unifiable terms.

The resolution principle extends the ground resolution principle as follows:

> *Choose any two clauses C_1 and C_2 in a set of clauses. Rename the variables in these clauses uniquely and so that no variable occurs in both clauses. Choose $D \subseteq C_1$ and $E \subseteq C_2$ such that each literal D_i in D is a negative literal, each literal E_j in E is a positive literal, and there is a most general unifier θ of all of the atomic parts of the D_i and all of the E_j. Add the resolvent $((C_1 - D) \cup (C_2 - E))\theta$ to the set of clauses.*

Robinson [166] proved the following theorem.

Theorem 1.6 *(Resolution Theorem.) A formula in clause form is unsatisfiable if and only if $\square$ is produced as a resolvent after a finite number of applications of the resolution principle.*

If a set of clauses is satisfiable, resolution may not terminate and may keep producing new clauses.

Using the clause form of F', choose the clauses $\{\neg q(a, w)\}$ and $\{q(x, g(x)), q(x, h(x))\}$. A most general unifier of the atom $q(x, g(x))$, and the atomic part of $\neg q(a, w)$ is is $\theta = \{a/x, g(a)/w\}$. The resolvent of the clauses is $\{q(a, h(a))\}$. Resolving this clause with

$\{\neg q(a, w)\}$ yields the empty clause. It follows from the Resolution Theorem that the negation of F is a valid formula, that is

$$\exists x \forall y \forall z \neg[(\neg q(x, y) \equiv \exists t[\neg \forall y(q(x, y) \supset \neg p(f(v)))]) \wedge \forall x \neg q(v, x)]$$

is a valid formula.

There are usually many ways to apply the resolution principle. We could have chosen the clause $\{q(x, g(x)), q(x, h(x))\}$ and formed the resolvents $\{q(a, h(a))\}$ and $\{q(a, g(a))\}$ by resolution with the clause $\{\neg q(a, w)\}$. The clause $\{\neg q(x, g(x)), \neg q(x, z), \neg p(f(a))\}$ and the resolvent $\{q(a, h(a))\}$ have resolvent $\{\neg q(a, g(a)), \neg p(f(a))\}$, which when resolved with the clause $\{q(a, g(a))\}$ yields $\{\neg p(f(a))\}$. The empty clause is the resolvent of this clause, and the resolvent of $\{\neg q(a, w)\}$ and $\{q(x, g(x)), p(f(a))\}$.

The resolution principle alone, although much more efficient than methods based directly on ground clauses, can still be inefficient because of the necessity to convert formulas to Skolem normal form, and because redundant resolvents can be produced. In general, propositional resolution has non-polynomial time complexity [80]. The length of a resolution proof for infinitely many disjunctive normal form propositional tautologies which are sets of "pigeonhole clauses" is not bounded by any polynomial function of the length of the tautology[2]. An extended form of resolution gives polynomial length refutations for such propositional tautologies. Urquhart [191] refined this result by using similar techniques on "graph-based" sets of clauses. Unlike pigeonhole clauses, they have polynomial length proofs in an axiomatic system for the propositional calculus, and each clause C_n contains three literals instead of n literals. More generally, Baaz and Leitsch [13] have shown that the length of a shortest resolution proof for first-order clauses may be non-elementary in the length of a shortest proof in a classical logical calculus.

Proof methods based on variations of resolution have been developed which reduce redundancy by extending resolution for languages with equality [167], or by specifying which clauses should be chosen and which literals in those clauses should be tested for unifiability [124]. The variations maintain the property that $\square$ is produced as a resolvent if and only if the negation of the original formula in clause form is unsatisfiable.

One of these is linear resolution [123, 126] which reduces redundancy by always using the previous resolvent as one of the clauses used to form the next resolvent. SL-resolution, introduced by Kowalski and Kuehner [117], is a modification of linear resolution in which just one literal per clause is selected for testing unifiability.

1.2 Logic Programming

Apart from its use for formalizing and automating mathematical proofs, logic is also used as a programming language. The idea to use logic in this way is stated to have occurred in 1972 during a visit by R. Kowalski from the University of Edinburgh to the artificial intelligence group at Université d'Aix Marseilles [34], although the idea had occurred earlier to P. Hayes [116].

---

[2]The proof of this result does not use clauses, but it can easily be corrected.

The form of logic programming principally considered used Horn clauses[3]. A Horn clause program is a formula each of whose clauses contain one positive literal. To show that a closed formula $\neg G$ of the form $\neg \forall x_1 \cdots \forall x_n . \neg (A_1 \wedge \cdots \wedge A_n)$, where the A_i are positive literals, is a logical consequence of a program P, a form of resolution called *SL-resolution* was used to show that $P \wedge G$ is unsatisfiable.

The formula G in clause form is called a goal clause and it is a clause consisting of negative literals. Clauses in a Horn clause program are sometimes called definite clauses, and SL-resolution for definite clauses is called SLD-resolution[4] [11].

In SLD-resolution, a goal clause of the form

$$\{\neg A_1, \ldots, \neg A_{i-1}, \neg A_i, \neg A_{i+1}, \ldots, \neg A_n\}$$

and a definite clause from P of the form $\{A, \neg B_1, \ldots, \neg B_k\}$ whose variables have been renamed so that they are distinct from those in the goal clause and where $k \geq 0$, are used to form the resolvent or goal clause

$$\{\neg A_1\theta, \ldots, \neg A_{i-1}\theta, \neg B_1\theta, \ldots, \neg B_k\theta, \neg A_{i+1}\theta, \ldots, \neg A_n\theta\}$$

where θ is a most general unifier of the *selected literal* A_i, and A.

An example of Horn clause program is the formula

$$\{\{reverse(nil, nil)\},$$
$$\{reverse(cons(X, Y), Z,), \neg reverse(Y, R),$$
$$\neg append(R, cons(X, nil), Z)\},$$
$$\{append(nil, X, X)\},$$
$$\{append(cons(X, Y), Z, cons(X, T)), \neg append(Y, Z, T)\}\}$$

In first-order classical logic, a definite clause of the form

$$\{A_1, \neg A_2, \ldots, \neg A_n\}$$

is equivalent to the implication $A_n \wedge \cdots \wedge A_2 \supset A_1$. In logic programming, such an implication is abbreviated to $A_1 :- A_2, \ldots, A_n$. Using this abbreviation, the previous program can be written

```
reverse(nil, nil).
reverse(cons(X, Y), Z) :- reverse(Y, R),
                          append(R, cons(X, nil), Z).

append(nil, X, X).
append(cons(X, Y), Z, cons(X, T)) :- append(Y, Z, T).
```

A Horn clause program written in this abbreviated form is called a logic program. Similarly, a goal clause of the form $\{\neg G_1, \ldots, \neg G_n\}$ is abbreviated to $:- G_1, \ldots, G_n$.

---

[3]Horn originally defined similar clauses consisting of negated equations and at most one non-negated equation [95].

[4]However, G.A. Ringwood [165] states that SLD-resolution is D. Kuehner's [119] SNL-resolution without factoring, and that its identification [116] with SL-resolution is widely held but of questionable historical accuracy.

1.2.1   Least Model Semantics

Since the denotations of constant symbols in every Herbrand interpretation for a formula are fixed, it is usual to characterize a Herbrand interpretation by the set of all ground positive literals for which it is a model. We shall call the characterization of a Herbrand interpretation which is a model for a formula, a *Herbrand model* of the formula.

A basic fact about Horn clauses [95] is that the intersection of two Herbrand models for a Horn clause formula is a Herbrand model for the formula. The intersection of all Herbrand models of a formula is a unique model called the *least Herbrand model.*

Unique models are necessary for Horn clause logic to be regarded as a programming language. The identification of the least Herbrand model for this purpose is supported by the following result [52].

Theorem 1.7 *A ground positive literal is in the least Herbrand model of a logic program if and only if it is a logical consequence of the program.*

The existence of the least Herbrand model depends on the fact that only Horn clauses are being considered. Makowsky [128] shows that if such generic models are required, then first-order Horn clause logic with equality is the most general form of first-order logic with this property.

If a clause were to contain a disjunction $A \vee B$ where A and B are positive literals, there may be no least Herbrand model. There could be a Herbrand model which contains A but not B, and vice-versa. Their intersection would contain neither A nor B, and it would no longer be a Herbrand model for $A \vee B$. Clauses with such disjunctions arise in automated theorem proving problems. The lack of a least Herbrand model is not critical in this setting. The aim there is to show the unsatisfiability of a set of clauses rather than to investigate their properties as a programming language.

1.2.2   Refutations and Answers

Logic programming also differs from resolution based theorem proving because usually all refutations are of interest not merely the existence of a refutation.

This is because answers can be extracted from their composition of all most general unifiers computed for each refutation using a goal G and a logic program. The composition is an answer substitution θ, and $\neg G\theta$ is a logical consequence of P.

For example, using the previous program, the goal

```
:- reverse(cons(1, cons(2, nil)), X)
```

results in a refutation whose answer substitution is a most general unifier of the disagreement set:

$$\{\langle reverse(cons(1, cons(2, nil)), t), reverse(cons(x, y), z)\rangle$$
$$\langle reverse(y, r), reverse(cons(x_1, y_1), z_1)\rangle$$
$$\langle reverse(y_1, r_1), reverse(nil, nil)\rangle$$
$$\langle append(r_1, cons(x_1, nil), z_1), append(nil, x_2, x_2)\rangle$$
$$\langle append(r, cons(x, nil), z), append(cons(x_3, y_2), z_2, cons(x_3, u))\rangle$$
$$\langle append(y_2, z_2, u), append(nil, x_4, x_4)\rangle\}$$

which has the component $\langle X, cons(2, cons(1, nil)) \rangle$.

Some logic programs also can generate several answers to the same goal. For example the goal

```
:- append(X, Y, cons(1, cons(2, cons(3, nil)))).
```

will produce four answers corresponding to the four possible values for X and Y such that Y appended to X is `cons(1, cons(2, cons(3, nil)))`. This immediately leads us to ask what can be computed using logic programs.

1.2.3 Computational Adequacy

A binary definite clause has the form $A : - B$, where A and B are atomic formulas. Tärnlund [189] has shown that every Turing computable function is computable by a logic program consisting of binary definite clauses[5]. Turing's Thesis [6] states that every algorithm can be programmed on a one-tape Turing machine.

If this is accepted, it follows that every effectively computable function can be computed by logic programs with binary clauses. This observation is also necessary for Horn clauses to be regarded as a programming language.

Many high-level programming languages provide abstractions such as modules, procedures, abstract data types, and polymorphism. Logic programs do not support most of these features directly because only first-order terms can be used as data structures. While such features do not change the computational adequacy of a programming language, they make programs more concise and easier to write and to understand.

1.2.4 Negation

Another feature not directly supported by logic programs is negation. It is often useful to find which relations do not hold [32]. Since Horn clauses are a subset of first-order logic, negation must be approximated.

The negation as failure rule is one such approximation. The resolution search space for a program P and a goal clause G can be organized as a tree called a *SLD-tree*. The goal clause is the root of the tree, and after having fixed a selected literal in a node of the tree, the children of that node are all goal clauses which can be formed by applying SLD--resolution. A SLD-tree has a *success branch* if it has a finite branch whose last resolvent is the empty clause. A SLD-tree is *finitely failed* if all of its branches are finite, and none is a success branch. A SLD-tree is a *fair SLD-tree* if in each infinite branch of the tree, an instantiated form of any literal in any node is the selected literal of a descendant node which has been formed after a finite number of applications of SLD-resolution.

If P is a Horn clause logic program, and G is a goal, the rule allows us to infer G from $comp(P)$ if and only if there is a finitely failed SLD-tree [11] for $P \cup \{G\}$, where $comp(P)$ is a formula produced from P.

---

[5]Lloyd [122], for example, surveys various characterizations of the computational adequacy of logic programming.

[6]Davis [44] gives an historical account of Turing's Thesis.

Clark [31] defined the *completion* of a logic program $comp(P)$. The soundness of the negation as failure rule is the theorem that if there is a finitely failed SLD-tree [11] for $P \cup \{G\}$ then $comp(P) \models G$.

The completeness of the negation as failure rule is the converse of this theorem and we shall present the main details of its proof.

We briefly recall necessary definitions. More details are given by Lloyd [122]. The formula $comp(P)$ is formed from a logic program P using the following rules. Let $p(t_1, \ldots, t_m) \Leftarrow A_1, \ldots, A_n$ be a clause in a logic program P, where $\Leftarrow$ stands for logical implication. Let $=$ be a new predicate symbol whose intended denotation is the syntactic identity relation. The first step transforms the clause into

$$p(x_1, \ldots, x_m) \Leftarrow (x_1 = t_1) \wedge \cdots \wedge (x_m = t_m) \wedge A_1 \wedge \cdots \wedge A_n.$$

where $x_1, \ldots, x_m$ are variables not appearing in the clause. Then if $y_1, \ldots, y_d$ are the variables of the original clause, this is transformed into

$$p(x_1, \ldots, x_m) \Leftarrow \exists y_1 \cdots \exists y_d ((x_1 = t_1) \wedge \cdots \wedge (x_m = t_m) \wedge A_1 \wedge \cdots \wedge A_n).$$

Suppose that this transformation is made for each clause which has the predicate symbol p in the head. Then we obtain $k \geq 1$ transformed clauses of the form:

$$p(x_1, \ldots, x_m) \quad \Leftarrow \quad E_1$$
$$\vdots$$
$$p(x_1, \ldots, x_m) \quad \Leftarrow \quad E_k$$

where each E_i is the body of a distinct transformed clause.

The *completed definition* of p is defined to be

$$\forall x_1 \cdots \forall x_n (p(x_1, \ldots, x_n) \Leftrightarrow E_1 \vee \cdots \vee E_k).$$

If an atom occurs in the body of a clause and its predicate symbol is q, and q does not occur as the predicate symbol of any clause in the logic program, then the completed definition of q is defined to be

$$\forall x_1 \cdots \forall x_m \neg q(x_1, \ldots, x_m).$$

The following are the equality axiom schemas. They are intended to restrict the interpretation of $=$ to the syntactic identity relation on terms.

1. For all pairs c, d of distinct constant symbols $c \neq d$.

2. For all pairs f, g of distinct function symbols,

$$f(x_1, \ldots, x_m) \neq g(y_1, \ldots, y_k).$$

3. For each function symbol f,

$$(x_1 \neq y_1) \vee \cdots \vee (x_m \neq y_m) \Rightarrow f(x_1, \ldots, x_m) \neq f(y_1, \ldots, y_m).$$

4. For each constant symbol c, and each function symbol f,

$$f(x_1, \ldots, x_m) \neq c.$$

5. For each non-variable term t such that x is a variable which occurs in t, $t \neq x$.

6. $x = x$.

7. For each function symbol f,

$$(x_1 = y_1) \wedge \cdots \wedge (x_m = y_m) \Rightarrow f(x_1, \ldots, x_m) = f(y_1, \ldots, y_m).$$

8. For each predicate symbol p,

$$(x_1 = y_1) \wedge \cdots \wedge (x_m = y_m) \Rightarrow (p(x_1, \ldots, x_m) \Rightarrow p(y_1, \ldots, y_m)).$$

Definition 1.8 The *completion of P* is denoted *comp(P)* and it is the collection of the completed definitions for each predicate symbol in P and the above equality axiom schemas.

The generalized completeness of the negation as failure rule is the following theorem.

Theorem 1.9 *If G is a logical consequence of comp(P) then every fair SLD-tree for $P \cup \{G\}$ is finitely failed.*

The proof of this theorem shows that if there is a fair SLD-tree for $P \cup \{G\}$ which is not finitely failed then $comp(P) \wedge \neg G$ has a model.

The definition of the domain of the model uses an equivalence relation on the set T of terms each of which is either

- A variable in $\mathcal{X}$.

- A constant symbol occurring in P, or

- is of the form $f(t_1, \ldots, t_n)$, for an n-place function symbol f which occurs in P and terms $t_i \in T$ where $1 \leq i \leq n$.

The symbols s, t, u and v possibly with indexes will be used to denote terms.

Lloyd [122] stated that Wolfram et al. [196] showed that the equivalence relation, $*$, simplifies the proof of the theorem. The equivalence relation $*$ is defined for all $s, t \in T$ by

$$s * t \text{ iff } (\exists n \geq 0): s\theta_0 \cdots \theta_n = t\theta_0 \cdots \theta_n$$

where the θ_i where $i \geq 0$ are idempotent most general unifiers formed on an infinite branch in a fair SLD-tree for $P \cup \{G\}$.

It is easy to verify that $*$ is an equivalence relation. Here is the proof of transitivity, which is the most complicated part. Given any three atoms or terms s, t and u, suppose that $s * t$ and $t * u$. We have $s\theta_0 \cdots \theta_n = t\theta_0 \cdots \theta_n$ and $t\theta_0 \cdots \theta_m = u\theta_0 \cdots \theta_m$ for some

$m, n \geq 0$. Without loss of generality we can assume $n \leq m$. By idempotence of the most general unifiers we have $\theta_0 \cdots \theta_n \theta_0 \cdots \theta_m$ is $\theta_0 \cdots \theta_m$. Now

$$s\theta_0 \cdots \theta_n \theta_0 \cdots \theta_m = t\theta_0 \cdots \theta_n \theta_0 \cdots \theta_m \text{ and}$$
$$t\theta_0 \cdots \theta_n \theta_0 \cdots \theta_m = u\theta_0 \cdots \theta_n \theta_0 \cdots \theta_m$$

Thus, $s * u$ and we have proved the transitivity of $*$. It also follows directly that the equality axioms are satisfied using $*$.

The model using the domain $T/*$ is then constructed. It leads to the contradiction that $\neg G$ is a logical consequence of $comp(P)$ and the conclusion that every fair SLD-tree for $P \cup \{G\}$ is finitely failed.

Corollary 1.10 *The following statements are equivalent:*

- comp$(P) \models G$.

- *There exists a finitely failed SLD-tree for $P \cup \{G\}$.*

- *Every fair SLD-tree for $P \cup \{G\}$ is finitely failed.*

Negation as failure has limitations as an approximation to negation. There are logic programs P containing negation in the bodies of clauses where G is a logical consequence of $comp(P)$ but the search tree of the resolution strategies used to prove the soundness of the negation as failure rule for such logic programs is not finitely failed [122]. Shepherdson [173] has commented that clarity is lost if a logic program P is to be regarded as an abbreviation for $comp(P)$. Providing a model-theoretic account of more general uses of negation remains an open problem [140].

1.3   Discussion

We have traced the development of logic programming from the application of the Skolem--Herbrand-Gödel Theorem to automated theorem proving using resolution. The existence of least model semantics, and the computational adequacy of Horn clause logic programming enable it to be considered a programming language. However, useful programming features such as negation must be approximated. Abstractions such as modules, abstract data types and polymorphism are also not directly supported.

A semantics of logic programs is based on model theory for first-order logic. This is largely because of the relation of logic programming to resolution theorem proving. Extensions to logic programming sometimes attempt to ensure that answers are logical consequences of a program or a formula related to it.

We shall consider extending logic programming to higher-order logic programming based on Church's formulation of the Simple Theory of Types [27]. The model theoretic issues discussed here will have a similar treatment. We have dealt in some detail with results in the development of logic programming, partly to motivate our approach to higher-order logic programming, and partly to clarify what seems to be essential to it.

1.4   Overview of the Book

Chapter 2. Simply Typed λ-Calculus. The simply typed λ-calculus will be used to define the syntax of higher-order logics. We define type symbols and terms before considering α-conversion, β- and η-reduction, and $\bar{\eta}$-expansion, combinations of these relations, the complexity of typed β-reduction, normal forms, and substitutions.

Chapter 3. Higher-Order Logic. We present the Higher-Order Skolem-Herbrand- -Gödel Theorem for a form of Church's formulation of the Simple Theory of Types [27] called the Clausal Theory of Types. The Theorem uses Henkin's Completeness Theorem [87] for validity in general models.

Automations of higher-order logic are reviewed, and the syntax and Henkin-Andrews general model semantics [5, 87]. We then define higher-order analogues of Herbrand interpretations called λ-models. The Theorem leads to a partial decision procedure for testing the validity of formulas. It can be automated by a generalizing resolution.

Chapter 4. Higher-Order Equational Unification. We define higher-order equational unification. It subsumes unification and matching of simply typed λ-terms at all orders, and the major forms and their complexities are presented down to the first-order cases. This chapter is largely self-contained and can be read as an introduction to these forms of unification. Section 4.1 is directly related to the Clausal Theory of Types; the later sections of this chapter can be read separately without losing much continuity.

Higher-order equational unifiability uses a definition of higher-order rewriting. We give soundness and completeness results for higher-order equational unification procedures which enable us to define higher-order resolution with built-in higher-order equational theories for Clausal Theory of Types formulas. These results link unification and general model semantics.

The later sections discuss higher-order unification and matching, second-order monadic unification, and first-order equational unification. In particular, the open problem of the decidability of higher-order matching and several approaches for its solution are presented. We give a higher-order matching algorithm which is sound and terminating. We also present a class of decidable pure third-order matching problems based on the Schwichtenberg-Statman characterization of the λ-definable numeric functions on the simply typed Church numerals, a class of NP-complete pure third-order matching problems using a reduction from propositional satisfiability, the Plotkin-Statman Conjecture in some detail, and we consider Zaionc's treatment of regular unification problems. All of these approaches suggest that the problem is decidable.

Chapter 5. Higher-Order Equational Logic Programming. We use higher-order equational unification, to generalize the resolution principle [166] to Clausal Theory of Types formulas, and prove a higher-order Resolution Theorem for this form of resolution. This provides a method for testing the unsatisfiability of Clausal Theory of Types formulas. We then define Clausal Theory of Types Horn clauses and show that they meet the programming language criteria of being computationally adequate, and possessing least models. This latter property implies that validity in the general sense for Clausal Theory of Types Horn clauses can be determined from a single general model. These results are then combined with the higher-order Resolution Theorem.

We also define the operational semantics of Clausal Theory of Types programs and show, using classical fixed point methods, its coincidence with the model-theoretic semantics presented in earlier sections. We conclude by discussing prototype interpreters for Clausal Theory of Types programs.

Simply Typed λ-Calculus

We present the simply typed λ-calculus, which will be used to define the syntax of higher--order logics. We define type symbols and terms before considering various relations on terms, normal forms, and substitutions.

2.1 Type Symbols

The type system is based on that of the Simple Theory of Types [27].

Definition 2.1 The set T of *type symbols* is the smallest set formed using the rules:

- An element of the set T_0 of *elementary type symbols* is a type symbol. In particular, $\iota \in T_0$.

- If α and β are type symbols then $(\alpha \rightarrow \beta)$ is a type symbol.

Notation 2.2 Type symbols are written α and β possibly with subscripts. As an abbreviation, a type symbol of the form

$$(\alpha_1 \rightarrow (\alpha_2 \rightarrow \cdots (\alpha_n \rightarrow \beta) \cdots))$$

where $n > 0$ is written $(\alpha_1, \ldots, \alpha_n \rightarrow \beta)$.

Notation 2.2 differs from that in Church [27] and Andrews [7]. We write $((\alpha \rightarrow \beta), (\beta, \alpha \rightarrow \alpha) \rightarrow \alpha)$ rather than $\alpha(\alpha\alpha\beta)(\beta\alpha)$, for example.

Definition 2.3 The *order* of a type symbol is:

- $\forall \alpha \in T_0 : order(\alpha) = 0$.

- $order(\alpha_1, \ldots, \alpha_n \rightarrow \beta)$ where $\beta \in T_0$ is

$$1 + \max\{order(\alpha_1), \ldots, order(\alpha_n)\}.$$

2.2　Terms

The set C of *constants*, and the set X of *variables* are denumerable and disjoint sets. Each variable and constant is associated with a unique type symbol which is called its *type*.

From C and X, and the symbols $\lambda, ., (,$ and $)$, we inductively define a set T of *terms*.

Definition 2.4 The set T of *simply typed λ-terms* is the smallest set formed using the rules:

1. A variable is a simply typed λ-term. Two variables are identical if and only if their syntactic representations and their types are identical.

2. A constant is a simply typed λ-term. Two constants are identical if and only if their syntactic representations and their types are identical.

3. If $x \in X$ has type α and $t \in T$ has type β then $\lambda x.t \in T$ has type $(\alpha \to \beta)$.

4. If $t, u \in T$ have types $(\alpha \to \beta)$, and α respectively, then $(t\ u) \in T$ has type β.

A simply typed λ-term formed using rule 1 or rule 2 is called an *atom*, and one formed using rule 3 or rule 4 is called an *abstraction*, or an *application*, respectively.

Notation 2.5 For each type, the variables are written $u, \ldots, z, u_1, \ldots$ the constants are written $A, \ldots, Z, A_1, \ldots$. Terms are simply typed λ-terms. They are denoted by

$$p, q, r, s, t, p_1, q_1 \ldots$$

The type of a term t is written $\tau(t)$. An application of the form $((\lambda x.s)\ t)$ is abbreviated to $(\lambda x.s\ t)$.

The next definition is used to identify subterms of a term.

Definition 2.6 An *occurrence* is an element of the smallest set formed using the rules:

- ϵ is an occurrence.

- 0 and 1 are occurrences.

- If i and j are occurrences, then $i.j$ is an occurrence.

- If i is an occurrence, then $i.\epsilon = \epsilon.i = i$.

- If i, j, and k are occurrences, then $(i.j).k = i.(j.k)$.

Remark 2.7 The set of occurrences in Definition 2.6 forms a monoid with . as multiplication and ϵ as identity.

The following definition generalizes that for first-order terms[1] [100].

---

[1] Section 3.1, page 807.

Definition 2.8 The *set of occurrences* of a term t, $\mathcal{O}(t)$, and the *subterm of t at occurrence i, t/i*, where $i \in \mathcal{O}(t)$ are defined by:

1. For every term t, $\epsilon \in \mathcal{O}(t)$, and $t/\epsilon = t$.

2. If t is a variable or a constant, then $\mathcal{O}(t) = \{\epsilon\}$.

3. If t has the form $\lambda x.r$, then

$$\mathcal{O}(t) = \{\epsilon\} \cup \{0.l \mid l \in \mathcal{O}(r)\}$$

   and $t/0.l = r/l$.

4. If t has the form $(s_0 \ s_1)$, then

$$\mathcal{O}(t) = \{\epsilon\} \cup \{0.l \mid l \in \mathcal{O}(s_0)\} \cup \{1.l \mid l \in \mathcal{O}(s_1)\},$$

   $t/0.l = s_0/l$, and $t/1.l = s_1/l$.

Example 2.9 Here are four examples of sets of occurrences of terms using Definition 2.8.

$$\begin{aligned}
\mathcal{O}(u) &= \{\epsilon\} \\
\mathcal{O}(\lambda u.(\lambda v.w)) &= \{\epsilon, 0, 0.0\} \\
\mathcal{O}(\lambda v.(u \ v)) &= \{\epsilon, 0, 0.0, 0.1\} \\
\mathcal{O}(\lambda u.(\lambda v.(u \ v))) &= \{\epsilon, 0, 0.0, 0.0.0, 0.0.1\} \quad \bigcirc
\end{aligned}$$

Example 2.10 Here are two examples of subterms at occurrences using Definition 2.8.

$$\lambda u.(\lambda v.(u \ v))/0.0.1 = v$$

$$\lambda u.(\lambda z.(\lambda v.(z \ v) \ (u \ w)))/0.0.0.0.1 = \lambda v.(z \ v)/0.1 = v \quad \bigcirc$$

Definition 2.11 Term s *occurs in* term t if and only if there is $i \in \mathcal{O}(t)$ such that t/i is s. Term s is a *subterm* of term t if and only if s occurs in t.

Definition 2.12 For every $t \in \mathcal{T}$ the set $\mathcal{OF}(t)$ of *occurrences of free variables* is the set of $i \in \mathcal{O}(t)$ which satisfy the condition:

$$((t/i = x) \wedge (\neg \exists k \in \mathcal{O}(t) : (i = k.l) \wedge (t/k \text{ has the form } \lambda x.s))).$$

The set $\mathcal{F}(t)$ of *free variables of t* is $\mathcal{F}(t) = \{t/i \mid i \in \mathcal{OF}(t)\}$. A variable x is a *free variable* of a term t if $\exists i \in \mathcal{OF}(t) : t/i = x$. A variable x is a *bound variable* of a term t if $\exists i \in \mathcal{O}(t) : ((t/i = x) \wedge (i \notin \mathcal{OF}(t)))$.

Example 2.13 Here are two examples of occurrences of free variables, using Definition 2.12.

$$\mathcal{OF}(\lambda u.(\lambda v.w)) = \{0.0\}$$

$$\mathcal{OF}(\lambda u.(\lambda z.(w \ \lambda x.y) \ u)) = \{0.0.0.0, 0.0.0.1.0\} \quad \bigcirc$$

Definition 2.14 For $i \in \mathcal{O}(t)$, $t[i \leftarrow s]$ where $\tau(t/i) = \tau(s)$ is

1. $t[\epsilon \leftarrow s] = s$ when $i = \epsilon$.

2.

$$\lambda x_1.(\lambda x_2.(\cdots \lambda x_n.((\cdots((t_1\ t_2)t_3)\cdots t_j)\cdots t_m)[j.k \leftarrow s] =$$
$$\lambda x_1.(\lambda x_2.(\cdots \lambda x_n.((\cdots((t_1\ t_2)t_3)\cdots t_j[k \leftarrow s])\cdots t_m)$$

when $i = j.k$ and $1 \le j \le m$.

Example 2.15 Here are two examples of replacements, using Definition 2.14:

$$\lambda u.(\lambda v.w)[0.0 \leftarrow x] = \lambda u.(\lambda v.x)$$

$$\lambda u.(\lambda z.(w\ \lambda x.y)\ u)[0.0.0.1 \leftarrow \lambda v.(w\ v)] = \lambda u.(\lambda z.(w\ \lambda v.(w\ v))\ u)\quad \bigcirc$$

2.3   Conversions and Reductions

We define relations on terms called α-conversion, and β- and η-reduction. These relations were named by Curry and Feys [39] for the untyped λ-calculus.

2.3.1 α-Conversion

Definition 2.16 The *replacement* of variable x by term s in term t is

$$t\{(x,s)\} = (\cdots(t[i_1 \leftarrow s])[i_2 \leftarrow s])\cdots)[i_n \leftarrow s]$$

where $\{i_1,\ldots,i_n\} = \{i \in \mathcal{OF}(t) \mid t/i = x\}$ and $\tau(x) = \tau(s)$.

Definition 2.16 does not depend on the ordering of $i_1,\ldots,i_n$.

Definition 2.17 For any $t \in \mathcal{T}$ such that t/i has the form $\lambda x.s$ where $i \in \mathcal{O}(t)$, if $y \notin \mathcal{F}(s)$ and $\forall j \in \mathcal{O}(\lambda x.s)$ such that $\lambda x.s/j$ has the form $\lambda y.r$ implies $x \notin \mathcal{F}(\lambda x.s/j)$, then the term $t[i \leftarrow \lambda y.(s\{(x,y)\})]$ is said to follow from t by the rule of α-*conversion*.

Definition 2.18 The relations $\triangleright_{1\alpha}$ and $\triangleright_\alpha$ are defined as follows:

- $t \triangleright_{1\alpha} s$ if s follows from t by the rule of α-conversion.

- $t_0 \triangleright_\alpha t_n$ if $t_0 \underbrace{\triangleright_{1\alpha} \cdots \triangleright_{1\alpha}}_{n} t_n$, where $n \ge 0$.

Example 2.19 Here is an example of α-conversion.

$$\lambda u.(\lambda v.(v\ u)) \triangleright_\alpha \lambda z.(\lambda v.(v\ z))$$

However, $\lambda u.(\lambda u.((v\ u)\ u))$ does not follow from $\lambda x.(\lambda u.((v\ u)\ x))$ by the rule of α--conversion. $\bigcirc$

Proposition 2.20 For any terms t, s, v, $\triangleright_\alpha$ has the properties:

Reflexivity. $t \triangleright_\alpha t$.

Symmetry. $t \triangleright_\alpha s \Rightarrow s \triangleright_\alpha t$.

Transitivity. $(t \triangleright_\alpha s) \wedge (s \triangleright_\alpha v) \Rightarrow t \triangleright_\alpha v$.

The relation $\triangleright_\alpha$ is therefore an equivalence relation[2] on $\mathcal{T}$.

Definition 2.21 For any terms s and t, $s \equiv t$ if and only if s is syntactically identical to t.

2.3.2 β-Reduction

Definition 2.22 An abstraction of the form $\lambda x.r$ has a *capture free form* $\lambda u.p$ for a term s where $\tau(s) = \tau(x)$ if and only if

$$\lambda x.r \underbrace{\triangleright_{1\alpha} \cdots \triangleright_{1\alpha}}_{n} \lambda u.p$$

where $n \geq 0$ and $\forall i \in \mathcal{O}(\lambda u.p)$ such that $(\lambda u.p)/i$ has the form $\lambda y.t$ implies $(u \notin \mathcal{F}((\lambda u.p)/i)) \vee (y \notin \mathcal{F}(s))$.

If $\lambda x.r$ is not in capture free form for s, there are finitely many subterms of $\lambda x.r$ of the form $\lambda y.t$ in which x occurs bound by the binder of $\lambda x.r$ and y is a free variable of s. Using α-conversion can rename y and reduce the number of such subterms. We have the following proposition.

Proposition 2.23 Given an abstraction $\lambda x.r$ and a term s where $\tau(x) = \tau(s)$, there exists a capture free form of $\lambda x.r$ for s.

Definition 2.24 Let t be a term and t/i have the form $(\lambda x.r\ s)$ where $i \in \mathcal{O}(t)$. The term t/i is a *β-redex* of t.

Let $\lambda u.p$ be a capture free form of $\lambda x.r$ for s. The term $t[i \leftarrow p\{(u, s)\}]$ follows from t by the rule of *β-reduction*.

Definition 2.25 The relations $\triangleright_{1\beta}$ and $\triangleright_\beta$ are defined as follows:

- $t \triangleright_{1\beta} s$ if s follows from t by the rule of β-reduction.

- $t_0 \triangleright_\beta t_n$ if $t_0 \underbrace{\triangleright_{1\beta} \cdots \triangleright_{1\beta}}_{n} t_n$, where $n \geq 0$.

---

[2]The proof that $\triangleright_\alpha$ is symmetric is similar to the version for the untyped λ-calculus [91], Lemma 1.17.

2.3.3 η-Reduction

Definition 2.26 Let t be a term and t/i have the form $\lambda y.(s\,y)$ where $i \in \mathcal{O}(t)$, $\tau(s) = (\alpha \to \beta)$, and $y \notin \mathcal{F}(s)$. The term t/i is a η-redex of t.

The term $t[i \leftarrow s]$ follows from t by the rule of η-*reduction*.

Definition 2.27 The relations $\triangleright_{1\eta}$ and $\triangleright_\eta$ are defined as follows:

- $t \triangleright_{1\eta} s$ if s follows from t by the rule of η-reduction.

- $t_0 \triangleright_\eta t_n$ if $t_0 \underbrace{\triangleright_{1\eta} \cdots \triangleright_{1\eta}}_{n} t_n$, where $n \geq 0$.

2.4   Normal Forms

Definition 2.28 If for every $i \in \mathcal{O}(t)$, t/i is not a β-redex of t, then t is in β-*normal form*.

We can abbreviate terms in β-normal form

$$(\cdots((t_1\,t_2)t_3)\cdots t_m) \quad \text{by} \quad t_1(t_2,\ldots,t_m),$$

and

$$\lambda x_1.(\lambda x_2.(\cdots \lambda x_n.t)\cdots) \quad \text{by} \quad \lambda x_1 \cdots x_n.t$$

where the x_i are distinct variables.

Notation 2.29 Such terms have the form $\underbrace{\lambda x_1 \cdots x_n.}_{binder}\,\underbrace{@}_{head}\,\overbrace{\underbrace{(t_1,\ldots,t_m)}_{arguments}}^{matrix}$ where the binder or arguments can be absent, and $@$ is either a variable or a constant.

$head(t)$ denotes the head of a term t and $binder(t)$ denotes its binder.

Definition 2.30 Let t be a term and t/i be a term the form

$$\lambda x_1 \cdots x_n.@(t_1,\ldots t_m)$$

in β-normal form where $i \in \mathcal{O}(t)$, $\tau(@) = (\alpha_1,\ldots,\alpha_{m+k} \to \beta)$, and $k > 0$. The term t/i is a $\bar{\eta}$-redex of t.

The term $t[i \leftarrow \lambda y x_1 \cdots x_n.@(t_1,\ldots t_m,y)]$ follows from t by the rule of $\bar{\eta}$-expansion provided $y \notin \mathcal{F}(\lambda x_1 \cdots x_n.@(t_1,\ldots,t_m))$.

Definition 2.31 The relations $\triangleright_{1\bar{\eta}}$ and $\triangleright_{\bar{\eta}}$ are defined as follows:

- $t \triangleright_{1\bar{\eta}} u$ if u follows from t by the rule of $\bar{\eta}$-expansion.

- $t_0 \triangleright_{\bar{\eta}} t_n$ if $t_0 \underbrace{\triangleright_{1\bar{\eta}} \cdots \triangleright_{1\bar{\eta}}}_{n} t_n$, where $n \geq 0$.

Remark 2.32 In the following definitions and notations, χ stands uniformly for either η or $\bar{\eta}$, and χ-conversion means either η-reduction or $\bar{\eta}$-expansion.

Definition 2.33 If for every $i \in \mathcal{O}(t)$, t/i is neither a β-redex of t nor a χ-redex of t, then t is in $\beta\chi$-*normal form.*

Definition 2.34 The β-*calculus* consists of $\mathcal{T}$ and the transitive and reflexive closure of the relations of α-conversion and β-reduction. The $\beta\chi$-*calculus* consists of $\mathcal{T}$ and the transitive and reflexive closure of the relations of χ-conversion, and β-reduction. This relation is denoted by $\triangleright 1\beta\chi$ for a reduction or conversion of one β- or χ-redex.

Theorem 2.35 *(Strong Normalization.) For every $t \in \mathcal{T}$, there are no infinite sequences of the forms $t_0 \triangleright_{1\beta} t_1 \triangleright_{1\beta} \cdots$, or $t_0 \triangleright_{1\beta\chi} t_1 \triangleright_{1\beta\chi} \cdots$.*

Corollary 2.36 *Every $t \in \mathcal{T}$ has a β-, and a $\beta\chi$-normal form.*

The pre-1942 proof of the Strong Normalization Theorem by A.M. Turing appears in Gandy [68] [3].

In general, normalization is difficult; the problem is in the fifth level, $\mathcal{E}^4$, of the Grzegorczyk hierarchy [79, 168].

Theorem 2.37 *(Statman.) Finding a β-normal form of a term cannot be done in elementary time [183].*

A consequence of the next theorem is that normalized terms are unique up to α--conversion. The original version of the theorem is for the untyped λ-calculus [29]. The version of this theorem for the $\beta\bar{\eta}$-calculus is discussed by Huet [98].

Theorem 2.38 *(Church-Rosser.) The β-, and $\beta\chi$-calculi have the Church-Rosser property: for all terms $t_0 \in \mathcal{T}$, if $t_0 \triangleright t_1$ and $t_0 \triangleright t_2$, then there exists a terms t_3 and t_4 such that $t_1 \triangleright t_3$, $t_2 \triangleright t_4$, and $t_3 \triangleright_\alpha t_4$.*

Remark 2.39 Terms in $\beta\chi$-normal form can be abbreviated in the same way as those in β-normal form, and Notation 2.29 also applies to them.

Definition 2.40 For any two terms t_1 and t_2, the relation $t_1 =_{\beta\chi} t_2$ holds if and only if they have the same type, the $\beta\chi$-normal form of t_1 is s_1, the $\beta\chi$-normal form of t_2 is s_2, and $s_1 \triangleright_\alpha s_2$.

---

[3]Turing's manuscript of the Strong Normalization Theorem and its proof is in the Library of King's College, Cambridge. A more recent proof is by Andrews [3].

2.5   Substitutions

Definition 2.41 A *substitution* is a function $\theta : \mathcal{X} \to \mathcal{T}$ which is written in postfix notation, and where $\forall x \in \mathcal{X} : \tau(x) = \tau(x\theta)$.

Notation 2.42 The domain of a substitution θ is written $D(\theta)$.

Definition 2.43 If for all $x \in D(\theta)$, $x\theta$ is a variable which is not x, then θ is a *renaming substitution*.

Definition 2.44 The set of *introduced variables* of a substitution θ is

$$I(\theta) = \bigcup\nolimits_{x \in D(\theta)} \mathcal{F}(x\theta).$$

If $I(\theta) = \emptyset$ then θ is a *closed substitution*.

Notation 2.45 We write substitutions as $\gamma, \mu, \pi, \rho, \sigma, \theta$, possibly with subscripts. A substitution θ is represented by a set of the form

$$\{\langle x, x\theta \rangle \mid x \in D(\theta)\}.$$

Definition 2.46 Let V be any set of variables, and θ be any substitution. The *restriction* of θ to V is $\theta \lceil V = \{\langle x, x\theta \rangle \mid x \in D(\theta) \cap V\}$.

As a consequence of the Strong Normalization Theorem and the Church-Rosser Theorem, we can now use the definition of β-reduction to extend the definition of substitution to an endomorphism on $\mathcal{T}$.

Definition 2.47 The *instance* $t\theta$ of a term t by a substitution θ where

$$\theta \lceil \mathcal{F}(t) = \{\langle x_1, t_1 \rangle, \ldots, \langle x_m, t_m \rangle\}$$

where $\{x_1, \ldots, x_m\} \subseteq \mathcal{F}(t)$, is the β-normal form of

$$(\lambda x_1 \cdots x_m.t)(t_1, \ldots, t_m).$$

A *closed instance* $t\theta$ of a term t is one where $\mathcal{F}(t\theta) = \emptyset$.

Definition 2.48 A substitution θ is a *$\beta\bar{\eta}$-normalized substitution* if and only if for every $x \in D(\theta)$, $x\theta$ is in $\beta\bar{\eta}$-normal form.

Huet [98] proves that for any ordering $x_{j_1}, \ldots, x_{j_n}$ of $\{x_1, \ldots, x_n\}$ in the definition of instance above,

$$(\lambda x_1 \cdots x_n.t)(t_1, \ldots, t_n) \;\triangleright_\alpha\; (\lambda x_{j_1} \cdots x_{j_n}.t)(t_{j_1}, \ldots, t_{j_n}).$$

Definition 2.49 If σ and θ are substitutions then their *composition* $\sigma\theta$ is the substitution $\{\langle x, x\sigma\theta \rangle \mid x \in \mathcal{X}\}$.

Composition of substitutions is associative [98]. We shall also find it useful to refer to the following relations on substitutions.

Definition 2.50 Let V be any set of variables, and σ and ρ be any substitutions:

- (Equality.) $\sigma =_V \rho$ iff $\forall x \in V : x\sigma \vartriangleright_\alpha x\rho$.

- (Ordering.) $\sigma \leq_V \rho$ iff $\exists \mu : \sigma\mu =_V \rho$.

The simply typed λ-calculus is the syntactic basis of Church's formulation of higher-order logic [27]. We now consider higher-order logic and its relation to the Skolem-Herbrand-Gödel Theorem.

Higher-Order Logic

We present the Higher-Order Skolem-Herbrand-Gödel Theorem for the Clausal Theory of Types. This is a form of Church's formulation of the Simple Theory of Types [27]. The Theorem uses Henkin's Completeness Theorem [87] for validity in general models.

We begin by reviewing automations of higher-order logic, its syntax using the simply typed λ-calculus, and Henkin-Andrews general model semantics [5, 87]. We introduce higher-order analogues of Herbrand interpretations called λ-models. We then define the Clausal Theory of Types as a sub-logic of the Simple Theory of Types with equality, and show that a higher-order Skolem-Herbrand-Gödel Theorem holds for it.

The Theorem leads to a partial decision procedure for testing the validity of formulas. It can be automated by generalizing resolution.

3.1 Automating Higher-Order Logic

Simple Type Theory[1] derives from the Ramified Theory of Types and was intended to formalize mathematical reasoning. Church [27] presented a λ-calculus formulation of simple type theory and used it to prove the deduction theorem, Peano's postulates for arithmetic, and a formalization of definition by primitive recursion.

More recent applications of logics which are based on this higher-order logic are in the areas of theorem proving, hardware verification, programming language design, automating Zermelo-Fränkel set theory, natural language processing, and program transformation.

The theorem prover *TPS* [9, 10, 136], uses Church's formulation of higher-order logic. The most recent version, called TPS3, uses expansion tree proofs [134], Huet's higher--order unification procedure [97], and tactics [78, 150]. An earlier version [9] was able to prove automatically a theorem of G. Cantor that every nonempty set has more subsets than elements.

Isabelle [149] is a higher-order logic theorem prover which is based on composing natural deduction inference rules [161] by higher-order unification. It can be used to represent and prove theorems in P. Martin-Löf's constructive type theory [129, 149], first--order logic, and other logics [151]. Isabelle derives subgoals using tactics and tacticals, as in LCF [78, 150] from which it draws ideas.

---

[1]Church notes [27, 28] that the Simple Theory of Types was suggested as a modification of A.N. Whitehead and B. Russell's [194] ramified theory of types by L. Chwistek [30] in 1921 and 1922 and by F.P. Ramsey [164] in 1926. The modification does not have axioms of reducibility [28, 194].

The *HOL* proof generating system [77] is a higher-order logic theorem prover which is implemented using Cambridge LCF [150]. It is used to model and verify hardware and it has been used to verify the correctness of a microprocessor [33]. HOL uses first-order matching to implement rewriting, and it does not use higher-order unification. Type symbols, constant symbols, and axioms are introduced using a hierarchy of theories. As in LCF and Isabelle, tactics and tacticals are used to produce subgoals.

Theorem proving systems for higher-order logics include the Edinburgh Logical Framework [12] which is based on a constructive type theory, Lego [83] which implements the Calculus of Constructions [37] which formalizes natural deduction proofs in an extension of Church's formulation of the Simple Theory of Types, and Nuprl [35] which is based on one of Martin-Löf's type theories [129].

The logic of *IMPS* or the Interactive Mathematical Proof System [57] is based on a form of Church's Simple Theory of Types which has partial functions and subtypes [54]. It is sound and complete with respect to a form of Henkin-Andrews general models, and is intended as a foundation for automating mathematical reasoning.

EKL [112] is a higher-order logic theorem prover which uses rewriting with higher-order matching. It has been used to prove Ramsey's Theorem and to verify the correctness of LISP functions.

The proof development system *Watson* [36] uses an axiomatization of Zermelo-Fränkel set theory in higher-order logic to automate mathematical reasoning. Proofs are developed using rewriting. It has been applied to hardware verification and problems involving category theory.

Most functional programming languages allow higher-order functions for conciseness and for programming with continuations [86]. By analogy with functional programming, developing 'higher-order' extensions of logic programming [139, 143] or combining first--order functional and logic programming [45, 81], or first-order logic with higher-order functions [177] yields programming languages which are more concise and based on logic.

Higher-order definite clauses are used as the basis for the logic programming language $\lambda Prolog$ [135, 139, 143]. Inference with these clauses is based on a sequent calculus rather than resolution, and the axioms of functional extensionality are not assumed. Operationally, it has similarities to SLD-resolution [11] where Huet's higher-order unification procedure replaces first-order unification. The language has been used to encode natural deduction rules of inference [58]. It has also been used with higher-order definite clause grammars [137], and to represent and transform programs [138].

Despite concerns about its undecidability, it has been shown that higher-order unification permits conceptually elegant solutions to difficult problems [138]. The TPS [136] and Isabelle [149] theorem provers, which use higher-order unification intensively, spend more time searching for proofs than searching for higher-order unifiers. A decidable form of higher-order unification has been defined and used in a logic programming language [135].

Incorporating higher-order extensions in Prolog [32] has been considered to be unnecessary [193] because certain uses of predicate variables and λ-calculus terms can already be encoded, and these extensions make programs hard to understand: they become excessively abstract and use deeply nested expressions. This argument seems to be inappropriate because the encodings are not theoretically well understood [137], and they are insufficiently general [138]. It is necessary to study the underlying logic.

3.2 Higher-Order Logics

The λ-calculus versions of higher-order logic which we consider are based on Church's [27] formulation of the Simple Theory of Types. Other formulations of higher-order logics do not use λ-calculus notation: D.S. Scott [172] uses power sets and products as primitives, and discusses other notations such as the Mitchell-Benabou language which includes functions, products, and power types [107].

3.2.1 Syntax

Formulas of higher-order logics are defined as terms of the simply typed λ-calculus. The definitions of bound and free variables of a formula are identical to those in Definition 2.12 for the simply typed λ-calculus.

Definition 3.1 The set T_0 of elementary types includes the type o of propositions, and the type ι of individuals.

Definition 3.2 A *formula* is a term of type o. A formula t is a *closed formula* if and only if $\mathcal{F}(t) = \emptyset$.

Syntactic abbreviations are used to define the logical connectives from a finite set of primitive logical constants.

Definition 3.3 The set $\mathcal{C}$ contains the *logical constants*:

$$
\begin{aligned}
\top \quad & \tau(\top) = o \\
\bot \quad & \tau(\bot) = o \\
= \quad & \tau(=) = (\alpha, \alpha \to o) \\
\neg \quad & \tau(\neg) = (o \to o) \\
\supset \quad & \tau(\supset) = (o, o \to o) \\
\wedge \quad & \tau(\wedge) = (o, o \to o) \\
\vee \quad & \tau(\vee) = (o, o \to o) \\
\Sigma \quad & \tau(\Sigma) = ((\alpha \to o) \to o) \\
\Pi \quad & \tau(\Pi) = ((\alpha \to o) \to o).
\end{aligned}
$$

Definition 3.4 Every constant symbol in $\mathcal{C}$ which is not a logical constant is a *parameter*.

We shall find it useful to refer to certain subsets of $\mathcal{C}$, and terms constructed using constant symbols in such subsets.

Definition 3.5 A *signature* is a subset of $\mathcal{C}$ which contains the logical constants and a parameter of type α for every $\alpha \in T_0$.

Definition 3.6 A term t is a *term over* a set of constants $\mathcal{B}$, if and only if for every $i \in \mathcal{O}(t)$ such that t/i is a constant, $t/i \in \mathcal{B}$.

Definition 3.7 A *term of the Simple Theory of Types* is a simply typed λ-term over $\mathcal{C}$. A *formula* is a term of type o. A formula t is a *closed formula* if and only if $\mathcal{F}(t) = \emptyset$.

Definition 3.8 For every term t, $\mathcal{S}_t$ is the signature which contains

$$\{\top, \bot, =, \neg, \supset, \wedge, \vee, \Sigma, \Pi\} \cup \{c \mid \exists i \in \mathcal{O}(t) : t/i = c \in \mathcal{C}\}.$$

In the formulation of the higher-order logic $\mathcal{Q}_0$ [7], the logical constants are Q, and ι with type $((\iota \rightarrow o) \rightarrow \iota)$. Church [27] and Henkin [87] used the logical constants N, A, Π, and ι. Andrews' system $\mathcal{T}$ [3] uses $\neg, \vee$, and Π as logical constants.

3.3   General Models

We now present the semantics of the simply typed λ-calculus formulation of the Simple Theory of Types. The model theory we consider below is based on that of L. Henkin [87] as presented by Andrews [7]. Toposes are also used to interpret higher-order logics [61, 120].

Definition 3.9 A *frame* is a collection $\{\mathcal{D}_\alpha\}_\alpha$[2] of nonempty[3] sets $\mathcal{D}_\alpha$ called *domains*, one for each type symbol α. In particular, the elements of $\mathcal{D}_o = \{\mathsf{T}, \mathsf{F}\}$ are *truth values*, and the members of $\mathcal{D}_\iota$ are *individuals* . The domain $\mathcal{D}_{(\alpha \rightarrow \beta)}$ is a collection of functions from $\mathcal{D}_\alpha$ into $\mathcal{D}_\beta$.

Definition 3.10 A *denotation function $\mathcal{J}$* maps each constant symbol c to some element of $\mathcal{D}_{\tau(c)}$ of a frame which is the *denotation* of c.

In particular, we now define the denotations of the logical constants.

- The denotation $\mathcal{J}\top$ of $\top$ is T.

- The denotation $\mathcal{J}\bot$ of $\bot$ is F.

- The denotation of the parameter $=$ is $\mathcal{J}=$ in $\mathcal{D}_{(\alpha,\alpha \rightarrow o)}$ where for every $x, y \in \mathcal{D}_\alpha$,

$$(\mathcal{J}=)(x,y) = \begin{cases} \mathsf{T} & \text{if } x \text{ is } y, \\ \mathsf{F} & \text{if } x \text{ is not } y. \end{cases}$$

- The denotations of the other logical constants are the functions defined by the following tables.

x	$(\mathcal{J}\neg)(x)$
T	F
F	T

x	y	$(\mathcal{J}\supset)(x,y)$	$(\mathcal{J}\wedge)(x,y)$	$(\mathcal{J}\vee)(x,y)$
T	T	T	T	T
T	F	F	F	T
F	T	T	F	T
F	F	T	F	F

---

[2]This is standard notation [7] which abbreviates $\{\mathcal{D}_\alpha \mid \alpha \in T\}$.

[3]Meyer et. al [133] consider completeness in Henkin models with empty types. Mitchell [142] summarizes these and further results.

- The denotation of Σ is that function in $\mathcal{D}_{((\alpha \to o) \to o)}$ which maps a function in $\mathcal{D}_{(\alpha \to o)}$ to T if it is the function mapping at least one element of $\mathcal{D}_\alpha$ to T, and otherwise it maps that function to F.

- The denotation of Π is that function in $\mathcal{D}_{((\alpha \to o) \to o)}$ which maps a function in $\mathcal{D}_{(\alpha \to o)}$ to T if it is the function mapping every element of $\mathcal{D}_\alpha$ to T, and otherwise it maps that function to F.

Definition 3.11 An *interpretation* is $\langle \{\mathcal{D}_\alpha\}_\alpha, \mathcal{J} \rangle$.

Definition 3.12 An *assignment* is a function ϕ from $\mathcal{X}$ into a frame $\{\mathcal{D}_\alpha\}_\alpha$ such that for each variable x, $\phi x \in \mathcal{D}_{\tau(x)}$.

Definition 3.13 An interpretation $\langle \{\mathcal{D}_\alpha\}_\alpha, \mathcal{J} \rangle$ is a *model* over a signature $\mathcal{S}$ if and only if there is a binary *valuation function* $\mathcal{V}$ such that for every assignment ϕ and term t of type α, $\mathcal{V}_\phi t \in \mathcal{D}_\alpha$, and the following conditions are satisfied for all assignments ϕ and all terms over $\mathcal{S}$:

1. $\mathcal{V}_\phi x = \phi x$.

2. $\mathcal{V}_\phi A = \mathcal{J} A$ where $A \in \mathcal{S}$.

3. $\mathcal{V}_\phi (s\ t) = (\mathcal{V}_\phi s\ \mathcal{V}_\phi t)$.

4. $\mathcal{V}_\phi \lambda x.t$ is that function from $\mathcal{D}_{\tau(x)}$ into $\mathcal{D}_{\tau(t)}$ whose value for each element $z \in \mathcal{D}_{\tau(x)}$ is $\mathcal{V}_\psi t$ where ψ is an assignment which is identical to ϕ except that $\psi(x) = z$.

Definition 3.14 Let $\mathcal{M}$ be a model over $\mathcal{S}$, ϕ be an assignment into the frame of $\mathcal{M}$, and t be a term where $\mathcal{S}_t \subseteq \mathcal{S}$. $\mathcal{V}_\phi t$ is a *valuation* of t in $\mathcal{M}$. If $\mathcal{F}(t) = \emptyset$ then all such valuations are identical. We write $\mathcal{V}t$ and call it the *denotation* of t in $\mathcal{M}$.

Notation 3.15 A valuation function associated with a general model $\mathcal{M}$ is unique. It will be written $\mathcal{V}^{\mathcal{M}}$ where it is necessary to distinguish it from other valuation functions.

Definition 3.16 A model is a *standard model* if the domains $\mathcal{D}_{(\alpha \to \beta)}$ of the frame of its interpretation consist of *all* functions from $\mathcal{D}_\alpha$ to $\mathcal{D}_\beta$, and it is a general model if they consist of *some* such functions.

Andrews [7] (page 186) notes that not all frames belong to interpretations, and not all interpretations are general models. As an example of the latter, not every interpretation contains the identity function in $\mathcal{D}_{(\iota \to \iota)}$ which maps $\mathcal{D}_\iota$ onto itself, but in such interpretations $\mathcal{V}_\phi(\lambda x.x)$ where $\tau(x) = \iota$ is not defined[4].

The following definitions and notations are based on those for the Simple Theory of Types [7, 87].

---

[4]To be a general model, the interpretation must satisfy closure conditions which are defined in Andrews [4] (pages 390–391).

Definition 3.17 Let t be a formula, and $\mathcal{M}$ a general model over a signature $\mathcal{S}$ where $\mathcal{S}_t \subseteq \mathcal{S}$.

- t is *satisfiable* in $\mathcal{M}$ if and only if there is an assignment ϕ into $\mathcal{M}$ such that $\mathcal{V}_\phi t = \mathsf{T}$.

- t is *valid* in $\mathcal{M}$ if and only if for every assignment ϕ into $\mathcal{M}$, $\mathcal{V}_\phi t = \mathsf{T}$.

- t is *valid in the general (standard) sense* if and only if it is valid in every general (standard) model $\mathcal{M}$.

Notation 3.18 We write

- $\mathcal{M} \models t$ to indicate t is valid in $\mathcal{M}$.

- $\models t$ to indicate t is valid in the general sense.

Definition 3.19 A function f of type $(\alpha_1, \ldots, \alpha_n \to \beta)$ in a domain of a general model is *λ-definable* if and only if there is a pure closed term t whose denotation in that general model is f.

Results by Andrews [5] motivate our inclusion of the logical constant $=$ whose denotation is defined in Definition 3.10. These results show that the inclusion of $=$ ensures that axioms of extensionality:

$$\forall x (f(x) = g(x)) \supset f = g$$

where $\tau(f) = \tau(g) = (\beta \to \alpha)$, and $\tau(x) = \beta$, are valid in the general sense. This is necessary for Henkin's Completeness Theorem to hold [87].

The results also show that the relation $=$ is not λ-definable by $\lambda xy.\Pi(\lambda z.z(x) \supset z(y))$ where $\tau(x) = \alpha$, $\tau(y) = \alpha$, and $\tau(z) = (\alpha \to o)$, and that the axioms of extensionality are not valid even if the axioms for η-reduction are valid.

3.4   The Clausal Theory of Types

We now define a restriction of the Simple Theory of Types, called the Clausal Theory of Types. These restrictions are necessary for our higher-order Skolem-Herbrand-Gödel Theorem to hold. Their semantic motivation follows Theorem 3.44 below.

Definition 3.20 A *primitive symbol* of the Clausal Theory of Types is either a

- Variable;

- Logical Constant Symbol: $=, \neg, \supset, \wedge, \vee, \Pi$; or

- Parameter: a constant symbol which is not a logical constant symbol.

Definition 3.21 A *Clausal Theory of Types signature (CTT signature)* is the union of the set of logical constant symbols, and the set of parameters of the Clausal Theory of Types where for every $\alpha \in T_0$ there is a parameter of type α.

Definition 3.22 A *Clausal Theory of Types term (CTT term)* is a term in $\beta\bar{\eta}$-normal form each of whose symbols is either a primitive symbol of the Clausal Theory of Types, or an element of the set $\{\lambda, ., (,)\}$.

For all CTT terms t and for all occurrences i, $i.j \in \mathcal{O}(t)$, if $head(t/(i.j))$ is Π then $head(t/i)$ is Π.

Definition 3.23 A *Clausal Theory of Types formula (CTT formula)* is a CTT term of type o.

3.4.1 CTT and Higher-Order Logics

There appear to be no widely accepted criteria to determine when a logic is a higher-order logic. Perhaps a necessary criterion is that the subformula property does not hold for a logic in question, because it does not hold for several higher-order logics. This is not so because it does not hold for some first-order modal logics [59].

Some higher-order logics allow embedded and self-embeddable predicates, but the latter are definable in first-order intensional logic [16].

The existence of impredicative definitions in a logic also is not a criterion for deciding when a logic is a higher-order logic: they occur in the Calculus of Constructions [37], but not in a form of Martin-Löf's intuitionistic theory of types [129].

The Clausal Theory of Types has quantifiable variables whose type symbols can include o, and embeddable predicates. It is a 'higher-order' logic for these reasons and because the order of its quantifiable variables can be any positive integer, it has abstractions as terms, and equality between them. These attributes make it more concise than first-order clausal logic.

3.4.2 Normal Form CTT Terms

In a similar way to Section 1.1.2 on Skolem normal form of first order formulas, we discuss an algorithm which transforms a CTT formula to its normal form. Model-theoretic properties which are used in proving our higher-order Skolem-Herbrand-Gödel Theorem involve CTT formulas in this normal form.

Notation 3.24 When writing formulas, $\odot(A, B)$ will be written $(A \odot B)$ where $\odot \in \{=, \supset, \wedge, \vee\}$. Parentheses will be omitted from conjunctions and disjunctions with the understanding that $\wedge$ and $\vee$ are left associative. For example, $(a \wedge b \wedge c)$ stands for $\wedge(\wedge(a, b), c)$.

There are six stages for rewriting a CTT term into its normal form. In each stage, there is a finite number of rewrite rules each of which has the following form.

Definition 3.25 A CTT *formula rewrite rule* has the form $r \leftarrow s$ where r and s are formulas over a CTT signature $\mathcal{S}$, and $\mathcal{F}(r) \supseteq \mathcal{F}(s)$.

If t is a CTT term over $\mathcal{S}$, then it can be *rewritten* with such a rewrite rule provided:

- There is $i \in \mathcal{O}(t)$ such that t/i is not a variable, and $\tau(t/i) = o$.

- There is a substitution π such that $r\pi \triangleright_\alpha t/i$.

If these conditions are met then the rewritten term is $t[i \leftarrow s\pi]$.

We now give the stages for rewriting a CTT term to a normal form CTT term. Each stage consists of a list of formula rewrite rules. The stages are performed sequentially and during each one a term is sequentially rewritten with the formula rewrite rules of that stage. The order in which the formula rewrite rules are used in a particular stage is arbitrary. Moving to the next stage only occurs when no formula rewrite rules of the current stage can be applied to the rewritten term.

Definition 3.26 Let t be a CTT term over a CTT signature S. The *normal form transformations* are the following formula rewrite rules which have been grouped into six stages.

Remove redundant quantifiers.

- $\Pi\lambda x.r \leftarrow r$ where $x \notin \mathcal{F}(r)$.

Eliminate $\supset$.

- $(A \supset B) \leftarrow (\neg A \vee B)$.

Produce negated equations.

- $(\neg A) = B \leftarrow \neg(A = B)$.
- $A = (\neg B) \leftarrow \neg(A = B)$.

Move $\neg$ inwards.

- $\neg\neg A \leftarrow A$.
- $\neg(A \vee B) \leftarrow (\neg A \wedge \neg B)$.
- $\neg(A \wedge B) \leftarrow (\neg A \vee \neg B)$.

Distribute $\wedge$ over $\vee$.

- $(A \vee (B \wedge C)) \leftarrow ((A \vee B) \wedge (A \vee C))$.

Distribute $\wedge$ over $\vee$.

- $((B \wedge C) \vee A) \leftarrow ((B \vee A) \wedge (C \vee A))$.

At the end of this stage, parentheses within disjunctions are omitted. For example, $((a \vee (b \vee c)) \wedge ((d \vee a) \vee b))$ is written $((a \vee b \vee c) \wedge (d \vee a \vee b))$.

Example 3.27 The CTT formula $\Pi(\lambda x.\Pi(\lambda z.(\neg(p(x) \supset (r \wedge t(x))) = \neg s(y))))$ can be rewritten to the normal form CTT formula

$$\Pi(\lambda x.\neg(((\neg p(x) \vee r) \wedge (\neg p(x) \vee t(x))) = s(y)))$$

by using the normal form transformations. $\bigcirc$

Lemma 3.28 *Rewriting a CTT term to a normal form CTT formula using the normal form transformations always terminates.*

Proof: We prove that rewriting a term in each of the six stages in Definition 3.26 terminates.

There can only be a finite number of subterms of t of the form $\Pi\lambda x.r$ where $x \notin \mathcal{F}(r)$. Repeatedly rewriting with the formula rewrite rule of the first stage removes all of them.

Eliminating $\supset$ terminates because each application of the formula rewrite rule involved strictly reduces the number of times $\supset$ appears in the term being rewritten.

Producing negated equations using the formula rewrite rules of the third stage terminates because they strictly increase the scope of $\neg$ in equations.

Rewriting with any of the formula rewrite rules of the fouth stage must strictly reduce the sum of the number of symbols of all of its subformulas of the form $\neg A$ in the term being rewritten.

The left side of the formula rewrite rule in the fifth stage matches a formula of the form $(A \vee (B \wedge C))$ The number of such formulas in the term being rewritten which have the same number of symbols as the matched formula strictly decreases with each rewriting using the formula rewrite rule of this stage. A similar observation holds for the sixth stage. $\square$

Definition 3.29 A *literal* over a CTT signature $\mathcal{S}$ is a normal form CTT formula over $\mathcal{S} - \{\Pi\}$ whose head is either $=$, $\neg$, a variable, or a parameter.

A *positive literal* has the form r where r does not have the form $\neg r'$. A *negative literal* has the form $\neg r$ where r is a positive literal. A literal is either a positive literal or a negative literal.

Example 3.30 The following terms are literals.

$$d(w(\lambda v.w(\lambda x.a, v), a), \lambda y.a, b(a, a)), \quad \neg d(a, \lambda y.y, x),$$
$$\neg(b(a, v(\lambda x.x)) = c(a, c(a, a))), \quad b(w(\lambda uv.v(u(x)), x), z)$$

where a, b, c, d are parameters, $\tau(c) = (\iota, \iota \to \alpha)$, $\tau(a) = \iota$, $\tau(d) = (\iota, (\iota \to \iota), \alpha \to o)$, $\tau(b) = (\iota, \iota \to \alpha)$, $\tau(x) = \alpha$, $\tau(y) = \iota$, and $\alpha \in T_0 - \{o\}$. $\bigcirc$

Subformulas of normal form CTT formulas are in a conjunctive normal form, which we now define.

Definition 3.31 A CTT formula over a signature $\mathcal{S} - \{\Pi\}$ is in *conjunctive normal form* if it has the form

$$(c_1 \wedge c_2 \wedge \cdots \wedge c_m)$$

where $m \geq 1$ and each c_i has the form

$$(b_{i,1} \vee \cdots \vee b_{i,n_i})$$

for all $i : 1 \leq i \leq m$, $n_i \geq 1$, and the $b_{i,j}$ are literals where $1 \leq j \leq n_i$.

Definition 3.32 A *normal form CTT formula* is a formula over a CTT signature $\mathcal{S}$ which has the form

$$\Pi(\lambda x_1.\Pi(\lambda x_2.\cdots\Pi(\lambda x_n.r)\cdots))$$

where r is a CTT formula over $\mathcal{S}-\{\Pi\}$ which is in conjunctive normal form, $\{x_1,\ldots,x_n\} \subseteq \mathcal{F}(r)$, and $|\{x_1,\ldots,x_n\}| = n$.

The next lemma will be used to show that there is no loss of generality if we only consider normal form CTT formulas.

Lemma 3.33 *Let t be a CTT formula and t' be the normal form CTT formula formed from t by applying the normal form transformations. The formula t is valid in the general sense if and only if t' is valid in the general sense.*

Proof: Let $r \leftarrow s$ be a formula rewrite rule in Definition 3.26, and suppose that $r\pi$ matches a subterm in accordance with Definition 3.25. The equation $r\pi = s\pi$ is valid in the general sense [7].

If t_1 is the formula formed by rewriting with $r \leftarrow s$, then by the first part of Andrews' Soundness Theorem [7], t_1 is valid in the general sense. The result follows by induction on the number of rewritings used to form t', which must be a finite number by Lemma 3.28, and because the validity of a disjunction of literals is independent of how its subformulas are parenthesized. $\square$

3.5   Term Structures

We shall formulate a higher-order analogue of the Skolem-Herbrand-Gödel Theorem, which was discussed in Section 1.1.1. We recall that the Theorem depends on four others, one of which, Theorem 1.2, uses Herbrand or free models.

Remark 3.34 We shall assume from now on that in every general model the denotation of any parameter does not depend on the extensional properties of its arguments but is merely a function of their valuations. This prevents the denotation of a parameter from being defined in a similar way to that of Π, for example.

A λ-model is our higher-order analogue of a Herbrand model. If restricted to first--order logic, it corresponds to a Herbrand model. We present higher-order formulations of Theorem 1.2 using λ-models.

Definition 3.35 Let $\mathcal{M} = \langle \{\mathcal{D}_\alpha^\mathcal{M}\}_\alpha, \mathcal{J}^\mathcal{M}\rangle$ be a general model over a CTT signature $\mathcal{S}$. The *term structure induced by $\mathcal{M}$* is $\mathcal{T}(\mathcal{M}) = \{\mathcal{E}_\alpha\}_\alpha$ where each set $\mathcal{E}_\alpha$ is a partitioning of closed CTT terms of type α over $\mathcal{S}$, and the following conditions hold.

1. $\bigcup_{d\in\mathcal{E}_\alpha} d$ is the set of all closed CTT terms over $\mathcal{S}$ of type α. If there is a term in this set which has a Π as a primitive symbol, then either α is o, or the term is the $\overline{\eta}$-normal form of that Π.

2. Two terms t_1 and t_2 of type $(\alpha \rightarrow \beta)$ are in a partition $d \in \mathcal{E}_{(\alpha \rightarrow \beta)}$ if and only if for all $e \in \mathcal{E}_\alpha$, and for all $s \in e$ if the $\beta\overline{\eta}$-normal forms of $(t_1\ s)$ and $(t_2\ s)$ are CTT terms, then there is $f \in \mathcal{E}_\beta$ and they are elements of f.

3. $\mathcal{H}$ is the set of all closed literals s over $\mathcal{S}$ such that $\mathcal{M} \models s$.

4. For every partition $e \in \mathcal{E}_\alpha$ where $\alpha \in T_0$, $t_1 = t_2 \in \mathcal{H}$ implies $t_1, t_2 \in e$.

5. $\mathcal{E}_o$ is $\{\mathcal{E}_o^\mathsf{T}, \mathcal{E}_o^\mathsf{F}\}$.

6. $\mathcal{H} \subseteq \mathcal{E}_o^\mathsf{T}$, and these conditions hold for all closed formulas over $\mathcal{S}$ of the following forms:

   - $r = s$ where $\tau(r) \in T_0$ is an element of $\mathcal{E}_o^\mathsf{T}$ if and only if r and s are in the same partition of $\mathcal{E}_{\tau(r)}$. Otherwise, $r = s$ is an element of $\mathcal{E}_o^\mathsf{F}$.

   - $r = s$ where $\tau(r)$ has the form $(\alpha \rightarrow \beta)$ is an element of $\mathcal{E}_o^\mathsf{T}$ if and only if for all $d \in \mathcal{E}_\alpha$ and for all $t \in d$ such that the $\beta\overline{\eta}$-normal forms of $(r\ t)$ and $(s\ t)$ are CTT terms, there is $e \in \mathcal{E}_\beta$ such that they are elements of e.

   - $\neg r$ is an element of $\mathcal{E}_o^\mathsf{T}$ if and only if $r \in \mathcal{E}_o^\mathsf{F}$. Otherwise, $\neg r$ is an element of $\mathcal{E}_o^\mathsf{F}$.

   - $r \supset s$ is an element of $\mathcal{E}_o^\mathsf{F}$ if and only if $r \in \mathcal{E}_o^\mathsf{T}$ and $s \in \mathcal{E}_o^\mathsf{F}$. Otherwise, $r \supset s$ is an element of $\mathcal{E}_o^\mathsf{T}$.

   - $r \wedge s$ is an element of $\mathcal{E}_o^\mathsf{T}$ if and only if $r \in \mathcal{E}_o^\mathsf{T}$ and $s \in \mathcal{E}_o^\mathsf{T}$. Otherwise, $r \wedge s$ is an element of $\mathcal{E}_o^\mathsf{F}$.

   - $r \vee s$ is an element of $\mathcal{E}_o^\mathsf{F}$ if and only if $r \in \mathcal{E}_o^\mathsf{F}$ and $s \in \mathcal{E}_o^\mathsf{F}$. Otherwise, $r \vee s$ is an element of $\mathcal{E}_o^\mathsf{T}$.

   - $(\Pi\ s)$ is an element of $\mathcal{E}_o^\mathsf{T}$ if and only if the $\beta\overline{\eta}$-normal form r of $(s\ t)$ is an element of $\mathcal{E}_o^\mathsf{T}$ for every closed term t such that r is a CTT term. If r is a CTT term and an element of $\mathcal{E}_o^\mathsf{F}$, then $(\Pi\ s)$ is an element of $\mathcal{E}_o^\mathsf{F}$.

Lemma 3.36 $\{\mathcal{E}_\alpha\}_\alpha$ *is uniquely defined.*

Proof: By the first condition of Definition 3.35, for all α the union of all partitions in $\mathcal{E}_\alpha$ is fixed. $\{\mathcal{E}_\alpha\}_\alpha$ therefore could only be non-unique if the partitions in a domain $\mathcal{E}_\alpha$ are not uniquely defined.

The partitions to which two closed CTT terms t_1 and t_2 over $\mathcal{S} - \{\Pi\}$ belong is unique where $\tau(t_1)$ and $\tau(t_2)$ are in T_0. If $\tau(t_1)$ is $\tau(t_2)$ then by all conditions of Definition 3.35 except the second, they are in the same partition if and only if $\mathcal{M} \models t_1 = t_2$.

If the closed term has type o and contains Π in it then by Definition 3.22 of CTT term, it occurs in a prefix and the term is a formula. This formula has the form (Πs) where s is a term of type $(\alpha \rightarrow o)$. By induction on the number of occurrences of Π in a formula, the partition to which the $\beta\overline{\eta}$-normal form of $(s\ t)$ belongs is unique for every closed CTT term t over $\mathcal{S}$ of type α. By the last part of the sixth condition of Definition 3.35, the partition to which $(\Pi\ s)$ belongs must also be unique.

The uniqueness of $\mathcal{E}_{(\alpha \to \beta)}$ follows by induction on types. Given that $\mathcal{E}_\alpha$ and $\mathcal{E}_\beta$ have been uniquely defined, suppose that there could be two distinct sets $\mathcal{E}_{(\alpha \to \beta)}$. To be distinct, in one of them a closed term t_1 is placed in the same partition as a closed term t_2, and in the other these terms are in different partitions. Since t_1 and t_2 can be in the same partition, it follows by the second condition of Definition 3.35 that for every partition e of $\mathcal{E}_\alpha$ and for all terms $s \in e$ such that the $\beta\bar{\eta}$-normal forms of $(t_1\ s)$ and $(t_2\ s)$ are CTT terms, there is a partition in $\mathcal{E}_\beta$ of which they are elements.

By the uniqueness of $\mathcal{E}_\alpha$ and $\mathcal{E}_\beta$, this property of t_1 and t_2 must also hold in the other form of $\mathcal{E}_{(\alpha \to \beta)}$. But by the same condition of Definition 3.35, t_1 and t_2 must be in the same partition. This is a contradiction that they are in different partitions. Therefore, $\mathcal{E}_{(\alpha \to \beta)}$ is unique. $\square$.

Notation 3.37 A partition in $\mathcal{E}_\alpha$ of the term structure $\mathcal{T}(\mathcal{M})$ is written $[t]$, where t is any term in that partition.

3.5.1 λ-Models

To form a λ-model induced by a general model over a CTT signature, each partition in each domain of the term structure is replaced by a function. We shall show that the resulting λ-model is a general model over the signature, and discuss its properties.

Definition 3.38 Let $\mathcal{M}$ be a general model over a CTT signature $\mathcal{S}$. The λ-model of $\mathcal{M}$, $\mathcal{N} = \langle \{\mathcal{D}_\alpha^{\mathcal{N}}\}_\alpha, \mathcal{J}^{\mathcal{N}} \rangle$, is defined from $\overline{\mathcal{T}(\mathcal{M})}$ as follows:

- $\mathcal{D}_\alpha^{\mathcal{N}}$ is $\bigcup_{t \in \mathcal{E}_\alpha} \overline{[t]}$ where

    - For $\alpha = o$, $\overline{\mathcal{E}_o^{\mathsf{T}}}$ is T, and $\overline{\mathcal{E}_o^{\mathsf{F}}}$ is F.
    - For $\alpha \in T_0 - \{o\}$, $\overline{[t]}$ is $\mathcal{V}^{\mathcal{M}}t$.
    - For $\alpha = (\beta \to \gamma)$, for all $[s] \in \mathcal{E}_{(\beta \to \gamma)}$, $\overline{[s]}$ is the function whose domain is $\mathcal{D}_\beta^{\mathcal{N}}$ and which maps each $\overline{[t]} \in \mathcal{D}_\beta^{\mathcal{N}}$ to $\overline{[r]}$ where r is a $\beta\bar{\eta}$-normal form of $(s\ t)$ and a CTT term.

- For all $c \in \mathcal{S}$, $\mathcal{J}^{\mathcal{N}}c$ is $\overline{[c]}$.

Remark 3.39 By Definition 3.20 of primitive symbols of the Clausal Theory of Types, and Definition 3.21 of CTT signature, $\overline{\mathcal{E}_\alpha}$ is not the empty set for any $\alpha \in T_0$.

Example 3.40 Suppose that $\mathcal{M}$ is a general model over a CTT signature $\mathcal{S}$, where $\mathcal{D}_\iota^{\mathcal{M}}$ is $\{1, 2\}$, $\mathcal{D}_{(\iota \to \iota)}^{\mathcal{M}}$ is the set of functions

$$\{\{\{(1,1),(2,1)\}, \{(1,2),(2,2)\}, \{(1,1),(2,2)\}\}\},$$

and a is the only parameter in $\mathcal{S}$ of type ι, and $\mathcal{J}^{\mathcal{M}}a = 1$.

Then $\mathcal{T}(\mathcal{M})$ contains the sets $\mathcal{E}_\iota = \{\{a\}\}$, and

$$\mathcal{E}_{(\iota\to\iota)} = \{\{\lambda x.x\}, \{\lambda x.a\}\}$$

The α-variants of $\lambda x.x$ and $\lambda x.a$ have been omitted in $\mathcal{E}_{(\iota\to\iota)}$.
$\mathcal{D}^\mathcal{N}$ contains the sets $\mathcal{D}^\mathcal{N}_\iota = \{1\}$ and $\mathcal{D}^\mathcal{N}_{(\iota\to\iota)} = \{\{(1,1)\}\}$. ◯

Definition 3.41 For all $f \in \mathcal{D}^\mathcal{N}_\alpha$, $\hat{f}$ is a closed CTT term t over $\mathcal{S} - \{\Pi\}$ of type α such that $\overline{[t]}$ is f.

Definition 3.42 Let $\mathcal{M}$ be a general model over a CTT signature $\mathcal{S}$, and $\mathcal{N} = \langle\{\mathcal{D}^\mathcal{N}_\alpha\}_\alpha, \mathcal{J}^\mathcal{N}\rangle$ be its λ-model. Let ϕ be an assignment into $\{\mathcal{D}^\mathcal{N}_\alpha\}_\alpha$, and r be a term over $\mathcal{S}$.
We define a valuation function $\mathcal{V}^\mathcal{N}_\phi$ as follows.

$$\mathcal{V}^\mathcal{N}_\phi r = \overline{[r']} \tag{3.1}$$

where r' is $r\{(y, \widehat{\phi y}) \mid y \in \mathcal{F}(r)\}$.

Theorem 3.43 *Every λ-model over a CTT signature $\mathcal{S}$ is a general model over $\mathcal{S}$.*

Proof: By Definition 3.38 there is a general model $\mathcal{M}$ over $\mathcal{S}$ whose λ-model is $\mathcal{N}$. Let ϕ be an assignment into $\{\mathcal{D}^\mathcal{N}_\alpha\}_\alpha$, and r be a CTT term over $\mathcal{S}$.
We now verify by structural induction on r, that $\mathcal{V}^\mathcal{N}_\phi$ satisfies the conditions in Definition 3.13 for an interpretation to be a general model.

- If r is a variable then by equation 3.1, $\mathcal{V}^\mathcal{N}_\phi r$ is $\overline{[\widehat{\phi r}]}$, which is ϕr by Definition 3.41, as required.

- If r is a constant, then by equation 3.1, $\mathcal{V}^\mathcal{N}_\phi r$ is $\overline{[r]}$, which by Definition 3.38, is $\mathcal{J}^\mathcal{N}_\cdot r$, as required.

- If r is an application of the form $(s\ t)$ then by induction, $\mathcal{V}^\mathcal{N}_\phi s$ and $\mathcal{V}^\mathcal{N}_\phi t$ exist. By equation 3.1, $\mathcal{V}^\mathcal{N}_\phi s$ is $\overline{[s']}$ where s' is $s\{(y, \widehat{\phi y}) \mid y \in \mathcal{F}(s)\}$. Similarly, $\mathcal{V}^\mathcal{N}_\phi t$ is $\overline{[t']}$ where t' is $t\{(y, \widehat{\phi y}) \mid y \in \mathcal{F}(t)\}$.

  By Definition 3.38 of λ-model, $(\overline{[s']}\,\overline{[t']})$ is $\overline{[r']}$, where r' is a $\beta\overline{\eta}$-normal form of $(s'\,t')$.

  We have $(s\ t)\{(y, \widehat{\phi y}) \mid y \in \mathcal{F}((s\ t))\}$ is

  $$(s\{(y, \widehat{\phi y}) \mid y \in \mathcal{F}(s)\}\ t\{(y, \widehat{\phi y}) \mid y \in \mathcal{F}(t)\})$$

  by Definition 3.12 of assignment.

  Hence, r' is a $\beta\overline{\eta}$-normal form of $(s\ t)\{(y, \widehat{\phi y}) \mid y \in \mathcal{F}((s\ t))\}$, so that $\mathcal{V}^\mathcal{N}_\phi(s\ t)$ is $(\mathcal{V}^\mathcal{N}_\phi s\ \mathcal{V}^\mathcal{N}_\phi t)$, as required.

- If r is an abstraction of the form $\lambda x.t$, then by Equation 3.1, $\mathcal{V}_\phi^\mathcal{N} \lambda x.t$ is $\overline{[t']}$ where t' is $\lambda x.t\{(y, \widehat{\phi y}) \mid y \in \mathcal{F}(\lambda x.t)\}$.

  For all $z \in \mathcal{D}_{\tau(x)}^\mathcal{N}$, $(\overline{[t']}\ z)$ is $\overline{[t'']}$ where t'' is a $\beta\overline{\eta}$-normal form of $(t'\ \hat{z})$, by Definition 3.38 of λ-model.

  But t'' is also $t\{(y, \widehat{\psi y}) \mid y \in \mathcal{F}(t)\}$ where ψ is identical to ϕ except that ψx is z. Therefore $\overline{[t'']}$ is $\mathcal{V}_\psi^\mathcal{N} t$, as required.

□

3.5.2 Properties of λ-Models

We now present the properties of λ-models used in proving the higher-order Skolem-Herbrand-Gödel Theorem. The properties follow from Theorem 3.44 below on the validity of normal form CTT formulas.

Theorem 3.44 *Let $\mathcal{M}$ be a general model over a CTT signature $\mathcal{S}$, $\mathcal{N}$ be its λ-model, and r be a normal form CTT formula. If r is satisfiable in $\mathcal{M}$ then r is satisfiable in $\mathcal{N}$, and if $\mathcal{M} \models r$ then $\mathcal{N} \models r$.*

Proof: The proof is by structural induction on r. Suppose r has the form $c(t_1, \ldots, t_n)$ where c is a parameter, and that there is an assignment ψ into the frame of $\mathcal{M}$ such that $\mathcal{V}_\psi^\mathcal{M} r$ is T, and r is unsatisfiable in $\mathcal{N}$. We shall show that this leads to a contradiction.

Define ϕv to be $\mathcal{V}^\mathcal{N}(\widehat{\psi v})$ for every variable v. By the proof of Theorem 3.43, we have that $\mathcal{V}_\psi^\mathcal{M} t_i$ is $\overline{[t'_i]}$ where t'_i is $(t_i\{(y, \widehat{\psi y}) \mid y \in \mathcal{F}(t_i)\})$ for $1 \le i \le n$. By structural induction on t_i where $1 \le i \le n$ and Definition 3.38, we have that $\mathcal{V}_\psi^\mathcal{M} t_i$ is $\mathcal{V}_\phi^\mathcal{N} t_i$. It also follows by the last part of that definition and from the assumption in Remark 3.34 above that $\mathcal{V}^\mathcal{N} c$ is $\mathcal{V}^\mathcal{M} c$ and the contradiction follows. Therefore r is satisfiable in $\mathcal{N}$, as required.

If $\mathcal{M} \models r$, suppose that there exists an assignment ϕ into the frame of $\mathcal{N}$ such that $\mathcal{V}_\phi^\mathcal{N} r$ is F. A similar contradiction follows by defining ψv to be $\mathcal{V}^\mathcal{M}(\widehat{\phi v})$ for every variable v, and showing that $\mathcal{V}_\phi^\mathcal{N} t_i$ is $\mathcal{V}_\psi^\mathcal{M} t_i$ where $1 \le i \le n$.

The other cases, where r has the form $s = t$, $\neg s$, $s \wedge t$, $s \vee t$, or $(\Pi\ s)$, follow directly.
□

Remark 3.45 In general, Theorem 3.44 cannot be generalized by allowing r to have the form $\Sigma(\lambda x.t)$ and $\mathcal{M}$ to be a general model over a signature which includes Σ. This is because there can be elements in the domain $\mathcal{D}_{\tau(x)}^\mathcal{M}$ which are not the denotation of any closed term. Theorem 3.44 provides a semantic motivation for the definition of the Clausal Theory of Types.

Definition 3.46 A *term relation* $\sim$ is an equivalence relation on the set of all closed terms over a signature $\mathcal{S} - \{\Pi\}$ and where $s \sim t$ implies $\tau(s)$ is $\tau(t)$.

A general model $\mathcal{M}$ over $\mathcal{S}$ is a *general $\sim$-model* over $\mathcal{S}$ if and only if for all closed terms s and t over $\mathcal{S} - \{\Pi\}$ we have $s \sim t$ implies $\mathcal{M} \models s = t$.

Notation 3.47 If $\sim$ is a term relation over a CTT signature $\mathcal{S}$, we abbreviate $(s,t) \in \sim$ by $s \sim t$.

Example 3.48 A subset of a term relation $\sim$ could be

$$\{(\lambda y.f(d,y), \lambda y.f(y,d)), (\lambda z.f(z,d), \lambda z.f(d,z)), (d,d)\}$$

where d and f have types ι and $(\iota, \iota \to o)$, respectively. $\bigcirc$

Definition 3.17 and Notations 3.15 and 3.18 of Section 3.3 are now adapted for λ-models.

Definition 3.49 Let t be a formula, and $\mathcal{M}$ a $\sim$-λ-model over a signature $\mathcal{S}$ where $\mathcal{S}_t \subseteq \mathcal{S}$.

- t is *satisfiable* in $\mathcal{M}$ if and only if there is an assignment ϕ into $\mathcal{M}$ such that $\mathcal{V}_\phi t = \mathsf{T}$.

- t is *valid* in $\mathcal{M}$ if and only if for every assignment ϕ into $\mathcal{M}$, $\mathcal{V}_\phi t = \mathsf{T}$.

Notation 3.50 A valuation function associated with a $\sim$-λ-model $\mathcal{M}$ will be written $\mathcal{V}^{\mathcal{M}}$ when it is necessary to distinguish it from other valuation functions.

Notation 3.51 We write

- $\mathcal{M} \models t$ to indicate t is valid in a $\sim$-λ-model $\mathcal{M}$.

- $\models_\sim t$ if and only if t is valid in every $\sim$-λ-model over a signature $\mathcal{S}$ where $\mathcal{S}_t \subseteq \mathcal{S}$.

Theorem 3.52 *If r is a normal form CTT formula then r is satisfiable in a general $\sim$-model over $\mathcal{S}_r$ if and only if r is satisfiable in a $\sim$-λ-model over $\mathcal{S}_r$.*

Proof: If r is satisfiable in a general $\sim$-model $\mathcal{M}$ over $\mathcal{S}_r$, then by Theorem 3.44, r is satisfiable in the λ-model $\mathcal{N}$ of $\mathcal{M}$. From Definition 3.46, if s and t are closed terms over $\mathcal{S}_r$ and $s \sim t$ then $\mathcal{M} \models s = t$. We also have $\mathcal{N} \models s = t$ by Theorem 3.44, so that $\mathcal{N}$ is a $\sim$-λ-model over $\mathcal{S}_r$ as required.

The converse follows because a $\sim$-λ-model over $\mathcal{S}_r$ is a general model over $\mathcal{S}_r$ by Theorem 3.43, and is a general $\sim$-model by Definition 3.46. $\square$

3.6   The Higher-Order Theorem

We recall from Section 1.1.1 the Skolem-Herbrand-Gödel Theorem:

Theorem 3.53 *(Skolem-Herbrand-Gödel.) A formula A is valid if and only if a compound instance of a Skolem normal form of $\neg A$ is unsatisfiable.*

Our higher-order analogue of the Skolem-Herbrand-Gödel Theorem applies to normal form formulas of the Clausal Theory of Types. Every CTT formula can be transformed to one in normal form by using the normal form transformations of Definition 3.26.

We now define analogues of Herbrand expansions and compound instances for these formulas.

Definition 3.54 Let r be a closed normal form CTT formula over a CTT signature $\mathcal{S}$. A *higher-order expansion* of r is a CTT formula which is defined as follows.

1. If r is a term over $\mathcal{S} - \{\Pi\}$ then r is its only higher-order expansion.

2. If r has the form $\Pi(\lambda x_1.\Pi(\lambda x_2.\cdots\Pi(\lambda x_n.t)\cdots))$ then a higher-order expansion of r is the normal form of $(t\theta_1 \wedge t\theta_2 \wedge \cdots)$ where for all $i : 1 \leq i \leq n$, $x_i\theta_j$ is a closed *CTT* term over $\mathcal{S} - \{\Pi\}$, and for every $j, k \geq 1$, $t\theta_j \rhd_\alpha t\theta_k$ if and only if $j = k$.

A *higher-order compound instance* is the normal form of $(t\theta_1 \wedge \cdots \wedge t\theta_m)$ where $m \geq 1$ and the θ_i satisfy the conditions on substitutions in the second condition above.

The closed literals in a higher-order expansion can be interpreted as propositions, as follows.

Definition 3.55 Let $\sim$ be a term relation on terms over a CTT signature $\mathcal{S}$. A $\sim$-*propositional interpretation* is a function $\varphi_\sim$ mapping the set of closed literals over $\mathcal{S}$ to $\{\mathsf{T}, \mathsf{F}\}$ which satisfies all of the following conditions.

1. $\varphi_\sim(s = t)$ if and only if $s \sim t$.

2. $\varphi_\sim \neg s$ is not $\varphi_\sim s$.

3. If $s \rhd_\alpha t$ then $\varphi_\sim s$ is $\varphi_\sim t$.

The following definition continues the analogy with propositional logic.

Definition 3.56 A higher-order expansion or compound instance of a closed normal form CTT formula over a CTT signature $\mathcal{S}$ which has the form

$$(s_{1,1} \vee \cdots \vee s_{1,n_1}) \wedge (s_{2,1} \vee \cdots \vee s_{2,n_2}) \wedge \cdots$$

is *propositionally $\sim$-unsatisfiable* for a term relation $\sim$ on terms over $\mathcal{S}$ if and only if there is no $\sim$-propositional interpretation $\varphi_\sim$ such that for each disjunction $(s_{k,1} \vee \cdots \vee s_{k,n_k})$ where $k \geq 1$, there is $i : 1 \leq i \leq n_k$ such that $\varphi_\sim s_{k,i}$ is T.

The following theorem links the propositional treatment of higher-order expansions and λ-models. It is used in a main step in the proof of our Skolem-Herbrand-Gödel Theorem.

Theorem 3.57 *There is a bijection between the set of all $\sim$-propositional interpretations of closed literals over a CTT signature $\mathcal{S}$ and the set of all $\sim$-λ-models over $\mathcal{S}$. The bijection is defined by $\varphi_\sim s$ is $\mathcal{V}^\mathcal{N} s$ for each $\sim$-λ-model $\mathcal{N}$ over $\mathcal{S}$, and all closed literals s over $\mathcal{S}$.*

Proof: We show that a $\sim$-λ-model $\mathcal{N}$ over $\mathcal{S}$ is characterized by the set $\mathcal{H}$ of all closed literals s over $\mathcal{S}$ such that $\mathcal{N} \models s$. The result then follows by defining $\varphi_\sim s$ to be $\mathcal{V}^\mathcal{N} s$. It is easy to verify from Definition 3.55 that $\varphi_\sim$ is a $\sim$-propositional interpretation, and that it is unique.

From Theorem 3.43, $\mathcal{N}$ is a general model over $\mathcal{S}$, and by Definition 3.46 it is a general $\sim$-model over $\mathcal{S}$. From Definition 3.35 and Lemma 3.36, it follows that $\mathcal{T}(\mathcal{N})$ is characterized by $\mathcal{H}$. We also have by Definition 3.38, that $\mathcal{J}^\mathcal{N} c$ is $\overline{[c]}$ for all $c \in \mathcal{S}$, so that the λ-model of $\mathcal{N}$ is $\mathcal{N}$. $\square$

The following corollary is a direct consequence of this result. It will be used to define higher-order analogues of the resolution principle.

Corollary 3.58 *For all term relations $\sim$ on terms over a CTT signature $\mathcal{S}$, the $\sim$-λ- -model over $\mathcal{S}$ is uniquely defined by specifying the set of all closed literals over $\mathcal{S}$ each of which has the denotation T in the model. The characteristic function of this set is the $\sim$-propositional interpretation which corresponds to the model.*

We now give the higher-order analogue of the Skolem-Herbrand-Gödel Theorem.

Theorem 3.59 *Let $\sim$ be a term relation on CTT terms over a CTT signature $\mathcal{S}$. A closed CTT formula over $\mathcal{S}$ is unsatisfiable in every general $\sim$-model over $\mathcal{S}$ if and only if it has a higher-order compound instance which is propositionally $\sim$-unsatisfiable.*

Proof: If the formula r is unsatisfiable in every general $\sim$-model over $\mathcal{S}$, by Theorem 3.52 it is unsatisfiable in every $\sim$-λ-model over $\mathcal{S}$.

Suppose that r has the form $\Pi(\lambda x_1.\Pi(\lambda x_2.\cdots \Pi(\lambda x_n.t)\cdots))$ where $n \geq 0$.

For each $\sim$-λ-model $\mathcal{N}$ over $\mathcal{S}$, we have $\mathcal{V}^\mathcal{N} r = \mathsf{F}$ and that there exist $y_i \in \mathcal{D}^\mathcal{N}_{\tau(x_i)}$ such that $(\cdots((\mathcal{V}^\mathcal{N} \lambda x_1 \cdots x_n.t\ y_1)y_2)\cdots y_n)$ is F, where $1 \leq i \leq n$. Let $\theta = \{(x_i, \widehat{y_i}) | 1 \leq i \leq n\}$, using Definition 3.41. It follows that $\mathcal{V}^\mathcal{N} t\theta = \mathsf{F}$, and that there is $k \geq 1$ such that $t\theta_k$ in the pre-normalized higher-order expansion $(t\theta_1 \wedge t\theta_2 \wedge \cdots)$ of r is $t\theta$. From Theorem 3.57, there is a $\sim$-propositional interpretation $\varphi_\sim$ which uniquely corresponds to $\mathcal{N}$, and t' is propositionally $\sim$-unsatisfiable where t' is the normal form of $t\theta$. Therefore, the higher- -order expansion of r is propositionally $\sim$-unsatisfiable, by Definition 3.56. It follows by the Compactness Theorem for propositional logic [7] that a higher-order compound instance of r is propositionally $\sim$-unsatisfiable.

To show the converse, if a higher-order compound instance of r is propositionally $\sim$- -unsatisfiable, then it follows immediately that the normal form of $(t\theta_1 \wedge t\theta_2 \wedge \cdots)$ is propositionally $\sim$-unsatisfiable. By Definition 3.56, for every $\sim$-propositional interpret- ation $\varphi_\sim$ there is $k \geq 1$ such that t' is propositionally $\sim$-unsatisfiable where t' is the normal form of $t\theta_k$. By Theorem 3.57, there is a $\sim$-λ-model $\mathcal{N}$ which uniquely corresponds to $\varphi_\sim$, and that $\mathcal{V}^\mathcal{N} t\theta_k$ is F. Suppose θ_k has the form $\{(x_i, t_i) | 1 \leq i \leq n\}$. It follows that

$$(\cdots(\mathcal{V}^\mathcal{N} \lambda x_1 \cdots x_n.t\ \mathcal{V}^\mathcal{N} t_1)\cdots \mathcal{V}^\mathcal{N} t_n)$$

is F, and that r is unsatisfiable in every $\sim$-λ-model over $\mathcal{S}$. By Theorem 3.52, r is unsatisfiable in every general $\sim$-model over $\mathcal{S}$. $\square$

Lemma 3.60 *The higher-order compound instances of a formula are recursively enumerable.*

Proof: This is immediate from the observation that the terms of the Clausal Theory of Types are recursively enumerable. □

Lemma 3.60 leads to a procedure which is similar to the one in Section 1.1.4. If the following procedure halts, the CTT formula

$$\Pi(\lambda x_1.\Pi(\lambda x_2.\cdots\Pi(\lambda x_n.t)\cdots))$$

over a signature $\mathcal{S}$ is unsatisfiable in every general $\sim$-model over $\mathcal{S}$.

- Repeatedly generate the next compound instance of

$$\Pi(\lambda x_1.\Pi(\lambda x_2.\cdots\Pi(\lambda x_n.t)\cdots))$$

  and test if it is propositionally $\sim$-unsatisfiable.

- If so, halt with the answer 'unsatisfiable'.

This procedure can be phrased also in terms of validity. Form the closure

$$\Sigma(\lambda x_1.\Sigma(\lambda x_2.\cdots\Sigma(\lambda x_n.t)\cdots)).$$

This formula is valid in every general $\sim$-model over $\mathcal{S}$ if and only if the procedure halts using the formula $\Pi(\lambda x_1.\Pi(\lambda x_2.\cdots\Pi(\lambda x_n.\neg t)\cdots))$.

Testing the $\sim$-unsatisfiability of a higher-order compound instance of a closed CTT formula does not seem to have been considered before. The analogous problem for first-order logics with equality can be solved in $O(n \log n)$ average time by the congruence closure method [145].

When a term relation holds between closed terms if and only if they have the same $\beta\bar{\eta}$-normal forms, propositional unsatisfiability of compound instances can be tested, and standard methods such as ground resolution [166] can be used. In this case, the procedure is a partial decision method for testing the unsatisfiability of CTT formulas.

To make testing propositional unsatisfiability more efficient by using a higher-order generalization of resolution, and also to build-in equational theories rather than have explicit axiomatizations of equality as part of formulas, we now consider higher-order unification and its generalizations.

Chapter 4

Higher-Order Equational Unification

We define and discuss higher-order unification with a built-in higher-order equational theory. It subsumes unification and matching of simply typed λ-terms at all orders, and we present the major forms and their complexities down to the first-order cases.

Other forms of unification, their properties or applications are discussed in surveys by Gallier [64], Gallier and Snyder [67], Jouannaud and Kirchner [108], Knight [114], Snyder [181], and Siekmann [175, 176], and in collections of papers [110, 111].

Higher-order equational unifiability uses a definition of higher-order rewriting which can also be used for proofs in higher-order equational logic. We give soundness and completeness results for higher-order equational unification procedures which enable us to define higher-order resolution for CTT formulas of all orders. These results link unification and general model semantics.

We show that pure third-order equational matching is undecidable by a reduction from Hilbert's Tenth Problem. We discuss the open problem of the decidability of higher--order matching. Several approaches for its solution are presented. We give a higher-order matching algorithm which is sound and terminating. We also present a class of decidable pure third-order matching problems based on the Schwichtenberg-Statman characterization of the λ-definable functions on the simply typed Church numerals, a class of decidable matching problems of arbitrary order, show that pure third-order matchability is NP-hard by a reduction from propositional satisfiability, discuss resolving the Plotkin--Statman Conjecture, and consider Zaionc's treatment of regular unification problems. All of these approaches suggest that the problem is decidable.

4.1 Higher-Order Equational Unification

We shall define higher-order equational unification with a built-in higher-order equational theory, and higher-order rewriting on which it depends [201]. The possibility of this form of unification is mentioned by Siekmann [175] who suggests that it may be decidable for some equational theories. Snyder [180] and Qian and Wang [163] have given sound and complete procedures for higher-order equational unification where the equational theory is a first-order one. They use a generalization of the elementary transformations for first-order unification discussed by Martelli and Montanari [130], which were used earlier

for higher-order unification [182], and first-order E-unification [66, 182], and rigid E-
-unification [65, 67]. Another generalization of higher-order unification is for the Calculus
of Constructions [152], and matching for such calculi [47].

Definition 4.1 An *equation* is a closed term of the form

$$\lambda x_1 \cdots x_n.s = \lambda x_1 \cdots x_n.t.$$

where s and t are in $\beta\bar\eta$-normal form. A conjunction of equations is an *equational theory*.

Notation 4.2 An equation $\lambda x_1 \cdots x_n.s = \lambda x_1 \cdots x_n.t$ will sometimes be abbreviated to
its matrix, $s = t$. An equational theory is written E. It is sometimes represented by a set
of such matrices.

Example 4.3 An instance of Gödel's recursion combinator [73] provides an example of
an equational theory E:

$$\lambda xy.R(x, y, \lambda uv.v) = \lambda xy.x \; \wedge$$
$$\lambda xyz.R(x, y, \lambda uv.z(u, u(v))) = \lambda xyz.y(z, R(x, y, z))$$

where

$$
\begin{aligned}
\tau(x) &= \iota \\
\tau(y) &= (((\iota \to \iota), \iota \to \iota), \iota \to \iota) \\
\tau(u) &= (\iota \to \iota) \\
\tau(v) &= \iota \\
\tau(R) &= (\iota, (((\iota \to \iota), \iota \to \iota), \iota \to \iota), ((\iota \to \iota), \iota \to \iota) \to \iota) \\
\tau(z) &= ((\iota \to \iota), \iota \to \iota)
\end{aligned}
$$

Its abbreviated form is

$$
\begin{aligned}
\{R(x, y, \lambda uv.v) &= x, \\
R(x, y, \lambda uv.z(u, u(v))) &= y(z, R(x, y, z))\}
\end{aligned}
$$

    To define higher-order equational unification, we firstly define a higher-order rewrite
relation. We also use Definition 2.44 of the set of introduced variables of a substitution.

Definition 4.4 Let p and s be closed terms of the same type in $\beta\bar\eta$-normal form. The
higher-order rewrite relation $p \longrightarrow_{[i, q=r, \pi]} s$ holds if and only if

- $q = r$ is an equation of the form

$$\lambda x_1 \cdots x_n.t_1 = \lambda x_1 \cdots x_n.t_2$$

- i is an occurrence in $\mathcal{O}(p)$ and $\tau(matrix(p/i))$ is $\tau(t_1)$.

- π is a substitution such that $t_1\pi =_{\beta\overline{\eta}} matrix(p/i)$.

- A $\beta\overline{\eta}$-normal form of $p[i \leftarrow binder(p/i).(t_2\pi)]$ is s.

A special case of the higher-order rewrite relation is Definition 3.25 of formula rewrite rule. Another special case is that defined by Nipkow [146]. It restricts the left side of an equation used in rewriting so that every free variable f in it is in a subterm of the form $f(x_1, \ldots, x_n)$ where the x_i are distinct bound variables. This ensures that the problem of finding a substitution similar to π above is decidable [135], and has linear space and time complexity [162]. The decidability of finding such a substitution in general is discussed in Section 4.3. The higher-order rewrite rules of Jouannaud and Okada [109] define higher-order constants by primitive recursion on constructors, and seem to be unrelated to the rewrite rules defined here.

Example 4.5 Here is an example of higher-order rewriting. Let

$$\lambda uvwxy.u(v, \lambda y_1 y_2.B(y_1, y_2), y) = \lambda uvwxy.w(\lambda u_1.u(x, \lambda x_1 x_2.x_1, u_1))$$

be an equation, and $\lambda xy.f(z, \lambda t.y(B(C, z)))$ be a term.

The substitution π is $\{\langle u, \lambda w_1 w_2 w_3.y(w_2(w_1, z))\rangle, \langle v, C\rangle\}$. The matrix of the left side of the equation after applying π is $y(B(C, z))$.

The matrix of the right side of the equation after π has been applied is the term $w(\lambda u_1.y(x))$, so that $\lambda xy.f(z, \lambda t.w(\lambda u_1.y(x)))$ is the rewritten term. $\bigcirc$

4.1.1 Higher-Order Term Rewriting Systems

We define below a higher-order term rewriting system. This generalizes the first-order case [104]. Among many potential applications, using higher-order term rewriting systems in first-order rewrite-rule based languages and theorem provers [69, 74, 147] would simplify their treatment of bound variables. Special encodings, and supplementary code for α--conversions and substitutions become unnecessary.

Definition 4.6 A *higher-order term rewriting system* is a set $\mathcal{R} = \{q_i \leftarrow r_i \mid i \in I\}$ such that for all $q \leftarrow r \in \mathcal{R}$, $q = r$ is an equation.

We now use Definition 4.4 of the higher-order rewrite relation to define reduction.

Definition 4.7 Given a higher-order term rewriting system $\mathcal{R}$, the *reduction relation* $p \rightarrow_{\mathcal{R}} s$ holds if and only if there is $q \leftarrow r \in \mathcal{R}$ such that $p \rightarrow_{[i,q=r,\pi]} s$ holds.

In Theorem 4.11 below, we relate higher-order equational deduction to higher-order term rewriting systems. Ten derived equality rules of the higher-order logic $\mathcal{Q}_0$ [7] are given below. They are the rules of inference for deriving an equation $s = t$ from hypotheses E.

Axiom. Provided that $s = t \in E$,

$$\overline{E \vdash s = t}$$

Reflexivity.

$$E \vdash s = s$$

Symmetry.

$$\frac{E \vdash s = t}{E \vdash t = s}$$

Transitivity.

$$\frac{E \vdash r = s, \quad E \vdash s = t}{E \vdash r = t}$$

Congruence.

$$\frac{E \vdash p = q \quad E \vdash r = s}{E \vdash (p\ r) = (q\ s)}$$

α-Conversion.

$$\frac{E \vdash s = t}{E \vdash s' = t} \text{ where } s \rhd_{1\alpha} s'.$$

β-Reduction.

$$\frac{E \vdash s = t}{E \vdash s' = t} \text{ where } s \rhd_{1\beta} s'.$$

$\overline{\eta}$-Expansion.

$$\frac{E \vdash s = t}{E \vdash s' = t} \text{ where } s \rhd_{1\overline{\eta}} s'.$$

Abstraction.

$$\frac{E \vdash s = t}{E \vdash \lambda x.s = \lambda x.t}$$

Replacement. Provided that $i \in \mathcal{O}(t)$, and $t/i =_{\beta\overline{\eta}} q$,

$$\frac{E \vdash s = t \quad E \vdash q = r}{E \vdash s = (t[i \leftarrow r])}$$

Notation 4.8 The relation that an equation $s = t$ is derivable from an equational theory E is denoted by $E \vdash s = t$, and it is called the *entailment* of $s = t$ from E.

We recall [100] that $\xrightarrow{*}_{\mathcal{R}}$ is the transitive and reflexive closure of $\rightarrow_{\mathcal{R}}$. This leads to the following generalization of the $\downarrow_{\mathcal{R}}$ and $\uparrow_{\mathcal{R}}$ relations.

Definition 4.9 For all terms s and t, $s \downarrow_{\mathcal{R}} t$ if and only if $s \twoheadrightarrow_{\mathcal{R}} p_1$ and $t \twoheadrightarrow_{\mathcal{R}} p_2$ and $p_1 =_{\beta\bar{\eta}} p_2$.

The relation $s \uparrow_{\mathcal{R}} t$ holds if and only if there is a term r such that $r \twoheadrightarrow_{\mathcal{R}} r_1$, $r \twoheadrightarrow_{\mathcal{R}} r_2$, and $r_1 =_{\beta\bar{\eta}} s$ and $r_2 =_{\beta\bar{\eta}} t$.

By continuing the analogy with the first-order case, we now define the confluence of higher-order rewriting system.

Definition 4.10 A higher-order term rewriting system $\mathcal{R}$ is *confluent* if and only if for all terms s and t, $s \uparrow_{\mathcal{R}} t$ implies $s \downarrow_{\mathcal{R}} t$.

The following theorem can be seen as showing that Definition 4.4 is an appropriate one for higher-order terms.

Theorem 4.11 *Let $\mathcal{R} = \{q_i \leftarrow r_i \mid i \in I\}$ be a confluent higher-order rewriting system, $E = \{q_i = r_i \mid i \in I\}$, and s and t be any terms which are in $\beta\bar{\eta}$-normal form. Then $E \vdash s = t$ if and only if $s \downarrow_{\mathcal{R}} t$.*

Proof: To show $E \vdash s = t$ implies $s \downarrow_{\mathcal{R}} t$, it suffices to show for each of the ten equality rules above that if the relation holds for the entailments in the hypotheses of a rule, then it holds for the entailment in the conclusion of that rule. An example is the β-Reduction Rule where we have $s =_{\beta\bar{\eta}} s'$, so that $s \downarrow_{\mathcal{R}} s'$ by Definition 4.9. It follows that $s' \downarrow_{\mathcal{R}} t$ by the confluence of $\mathcal{R}$. The only relatively difficult case is the Replacement Rule. We have $t/i \downarrow_{\mathcal{R}} q$ using Definition 4.9 because $t/i =_{\beta\bar{\eta}} q$. We also have that $q \downarrow_{\mathcal{R}} r$ by assumption, so that by the confluence of $\mathcal{R}$ it follows that $t/i \downarrow_{\mathcal{R}} r$. Hence, $s \downarrow_{\mathcal{R}} t[i \leftarrow r]$, as required.

To show the converse, it suffices to show $p \rightarrow_{[i,q=r,\pi]} s$ implies $E \vdash p = s$, where $q = r$ is an equation in the equational theory E. Suppose $q = r$ has the form $\lambda x_1 \cdots x_n.t_1 = \lambda x_1 \cdots x_n.t_2$, and π has the form $\{\langle y_i, s_i \rangle \mid 1 \leq i \leq m\}$. We can derive $E \vdash t_1 = t_2$ by repeated applications of the Congruence and the β-Reduction Rules.

The Abstraction Rule can then be applied m times to form

$$\lambda y_1. \cdots . \lambda y_m.t_1 = \lambda y_1. \cdots . \lambda y_m.t_2.$$

The Congruence Rule can then be applied m times to form

$$(\cdots (\lambda y_1. \cdots . \lambda y_m.t_1 \ s_1) \cdots s_m) = (\cdots (\lambda y_1. \cdots . \lambda y_m.t_2 \ s_1) \cdots s_m)$$

which after at least $2m$ applications of the β-Reduction Rule yields $t_1\pi = t_2\pi$.

If $binder(p/i)$ is $\lambda z_1 \cdots z_k$, then we can apply the Abstraction Rule k times to form

$$\lambda z_1. \cdots . \lambda z_k.t_1\pi = \lambda z_1. \cdots . \lambda z_k.t_2\pi.$$

Finally, the Reflexivity Rule can be applied to obtain $E \vdash p = p$, and this in place of $E \vdash s = t$ in the Replacement Rule and $\lambda z_1. \cdots . \lambda z_k.t_1\pi = \lambda z_1. \cdots . \lambda z_k.t_2\pi$ in place of $q = r$ in that rule yields $E \vdash p = p[i \leftarrow \lambda z_1. \cdots . \lambda z_k.t_2\pi]$. From Definition 4.4, and by repeated applications of the β-Reduction and $\bar{\eta}$-Expansion Rules we obtain $E \vdash p = s$, as required.
$\square$

If $\mathcal{R}$ is also a terminating higher-order rewriting system, Theorem 4.11 implies that higher-order rewriting can be used to decide the derivability of an equation from a higher--order equational theory.

We now use the definition of higher-order rewrite relation to define higher-order equational unifiers.

Definition 4.12 A substitution θ is a *higher-order equational unifier* or *E-unifier* of two terms p and s of the same type for an equational theory $E = \{q_i = r_i \mid 1 \leq i \leq n\}$ if and only if $p\theta \xleftrightarrow{*}_E s\theta$. where $\mathcal{R} = \{q_i \leftarrow r_i \mid i \in I\}$ and $\xleftrightarrow{*}_E$ is the reflexive, symmetric, and transitive closure of the higher-order rewrite relation of the higher--order rewriting system $\mathcal{R}$.

The definition of higher-order equational unifier is now extended to sets of pairs of terms.

Definition 4.13 A *disagreement pair* is a pair of terms $\langle s, t \rangle$ where $\tau(s) = \tau(t)$. A *disagreement set* W is a finite set of disagreement pairs. The set $\mathcal{F}(W)$ is $\cup_{\langle s,t \rangle \in W} \mathcal{F}(s) \cup \mathcal{F}(t)$.

Definition 4.14 An *E-unifier* of a disagreement set W is a substitution which is an *E*-unifier of every disagreement pair in W. The set of all *E*-unifiers of W is denoted $\mathcal{U}_E W$.

We conjecture that this set is recursively enumerable for every consistent higher-order equational theory. There are such enumeration procedures when the equational theory is a first-order one [163, 180]. The current lack of an *E*-unification procedure when E is a higher-order theory does not prevent the implementation of resolution theorem provers for the Clausal Theory of Types. Higher-order pre-unification, which is discussed in Section 4.2.2 below, and explicit higher-order theories can be used together instead. This combination is likely to produce redundant resolvents as in the first-order case [24, 156].

In later sections, we shall consider higher-order equational unification and matching problems of descending order. The order of a type symbol for unification problems is defined differently to the order of a type symbol of a simply typed term. Unlike the latter, it is unnecessary to distinguish the order of a subterm of type ι from the order of a subterm of another type in T_0.

Definition 4.15 The *unification order* of a type symbol is:

- $\forall \alpha \in T_0 : order_{unif} \alpha = 1$.

- $order_{unif}(\alpha_1, \ldots, \alpha_n \to \beta)$ where $\beta \in T_0$ is

$$1 + \max\{order_{unif}\alpha_1, \ldots, order_{unif}\alpha_n\}.$$

From this definition, we can now define the order of a unification problem.

Definition 4.16 The *order* of a unification problem on a disagreement set W is

$$\max\{order_{unif}\tau(y) \mid y \in \mathcal{F}(W)\}.$$

4.1.2 Soundness and Completeness

In this section, we show that a higher-order equational unification procedure has logical soundness and completeness properties if it enumerates a sound and complete set of higher-order equational unifiers. The result will be used subsequently to show that higher-order equational resolution is sound and complete.

The Logical Soundness and Logical Completeness properties relate the higher-order equational unifiability of two terms s and t to the validity of $s = t$ in all general $\sim$-models. For first-order terms, they respectively can be reduced to Plotkin's Correctness and Completeness conditions for building first-order equational theories into the rules of inference of a theorem prover [156].

Remark 4.17 Throughout this section where it is not stated explicitly, we make the following assumptions:

- The signature S is a CTT signature, (Definition 3.21).

- All terms are CTT terms over S, (Definition 3.8).

- All general models are general models over S, (Definition 3.13), and the assumption in Remark 3.34 applies to the denotations of parameters.

- The range of all substitutions is the set of all CTT terms over S, and all substitutions are $\beta\overline{\eta}$-normalized substitutions, (Definition 2.41, and Definition 2.48).

- E is an equational theory over S, and the matrix of each equation in E is a CTT literal, (Definition 4.1, Notation 4.2, and Definition 3.29).

- A relation $\sim$ is a term relation on closed terms over S, (Definition 3.46), where $s \sim t$ if and only if $E \vdash s = t$.

- If $E = \{q_i = r_i \mid i \in I\}$ then $\mathcal{R} = \{q_i \leftarrow r_i \mid i \in I\}$ is a confluent higher-order rewriting system.

- $\mathcal{T}_E$ is a higher-order equational unification procedure.

We shall also use the following notation.

Notation 4.18 Let W be a disagreement set. Then $\mathcal{T}_E W$ is the set of all recursively enumerable E-unifiers of W by a higher-order equational unification procedure $\mathcal{T}_E$.

Logical Soundness and Completeness

In this section, we relate the higher-order equational unifiability of a disagreement set to the validity of equations formed from its disagreement pairs. This can be seen as a generalization of Plotkin's Correctness and Completeness conditions for building-in equational theories in first-order resolution theorem provers [156] to a higher-order case.

Definition 4.19 T_E has the *Logical Soundness property* if and only if for every disagreement set W, every $\sigma \in T_E W$, and every $\langle p, s \rangle \in W$, there is a substitution θ such that $\sigma \leq_{\mathcal{F}(W)} \theta$ and $\models_{\sim} p\theta = s\theta$.

We shall use the following Theorem to give a condition for T_E to have the Logical Soundness property. Theorem 4.20 is a generalization of Birkhoff's completeness theorem for first-order equational logic [19]. If the higher-order rewriting system $\mathcal{R}$ in the seventh assumption of Remark 4.17 is terminating, then Theorem 4.20 and Theorem 4.11 imply that the validity in general $\sim$-models of an equation which is a literal is decidable.

Theorem 4.20 *Suppose that $s = t$ is a literal. $E \vdash s = t$ if and only if $\models_{\sim} s = t$.*

Proof: To show $\models_{\sim} s = t$, it suffices to show for each of the ten equality rules above, that if it holds for the entailments in the hypotheses of a rule, then it holds for the entailment in the conclusion of that rule. The only non-trivial case is that of the Replacement Rule. We have assumed from the hypotheses of that rule that $\models_{\sim} s = t$ and $\models_{\sim} q = r$, and that there is $i \in \mathcal{O}(t)$ such that $t/i =_{\beta\overline{\eta}} q$.

By structural induction on t, it follows that for all general $\sim$-models $\mathcal{M}$, and for all assignments ϕ we have $\mathcal{V}_\phi^{\mathcal{M}} t$ is $\mathcal{V}_\phi^{\mathcal{M}} t[i \leftarrow r]$, and from $\models_{\sim} q = r$ that $\mathcal{V}_\phi^{\mathcal{M}} q$ is $\mathcal{V}_\phi^{\mathcal{M}} r$. Therefore we have $\mathcal{V}_\phi^{\mathcal{M}}(s = t)$ is $\mathcal{V}_\phi^{\mathcal{M}}(s = t[i \leftarrow r])$. From $\models_{\sim} s = t$ it follows that $\models_{\sim} s = t[i \leftarrow r]$, as required.

To show the converse, if $\mathcal{F}(s = t) = \{x_1, \ldots, x_n\}$, then

$$\models_{\sim} \lambda x_1. \cdots \lambda x_n.s = \lambda x_1. \cdots \lambda x_n.t$$

From the bijection of Theorem 3.57 between $\sim$-propositional interpretations and $\sim$-λ-models, we have that there is a $\sim$-λ-model $\mathcal{N}$ such that for all closed literals p we have $\varphi_{\sim} p$ is $\mathcal{V}^{\mathcal{N}} p$. From Theorem 3.43, we have that $\mathcal{N}$ is a general model over $\mathcal{S}$, and by Definition 3.46 it is a general $\sim$-model over $\mathcal{S}$. By Definition 3.55 of $\sim$-propositional interpretation we have $\lambda x_1. \cdots \lambda x_n.s \sim \lambda x_1. \cdots \lambda x_n.t$. Hence, $E \vdash \lambda x_1. \cdots \lambda x_n.s = \lambda x_1. \cdots \lambda x_n.t$, by the sixth assumption in Remark 4.17.

We can derive $E \vdash s = t$ from this entailment by applying the Congruence Rule to it n times, followed by $2n$ applications of the β-Reduction Rule. $\square$

We define the Logical Completeness property of T_E using Definition 2.50, as follows.

Definition 4.21 T_E has the *Logical Completeness property* if and only if for every disagreement set W, if there is a substitution θ such that for every $\langle p, s \rangle \in W$ we have $\models_{\sim} p\theta = s\theta$, then there is $\sigma \in T_E W$ such that $\sigma \leq_{\mathcal{F}(W)} \theta$.

We conjecture that given any consistent equational theory E, there is a general way to form T_E so that it has the Logical Completeness property. Generalizing narrowing [105] may provide such a procedure.

We now define properties of a set of higher-order equational unifiers. By the next theorem, if T_E enumerates a set of unifiers with these properties, then it satisfies the Logical Soundness and Completeness properties discussed above. This result, in the case of Logical Soundness, is used later to show that resolution in the Clausal Theory of Types is sound.

Definition 4.22 Let E be an equational theory, and W a disagreement set. A set $\mathcal{T}_E W$ is a *sound and complete set of E-unifiers* for W if and only if it has the following properties:

Soundness. $\mathcal{T}_E W \subseteq \mathcal{U}_E W$.

Completeness. $(\forall \theta \in \mathcal{U}_E W) : (\exists \sigma \in \mathcal{T}_E W) : \sigma \leq_{\mathcal{F}(W)} \theta$.

When they are translated to our notation, Plotkin's Correctness and Completeness conditions [156] in the first-order case are the same as the Soundness and Completeness properties of Definition 4.22 above.

The following theorem relates properties of a set of E-unifiers to Logical Soundness and Completeness.

Theorem 4.23 *Let W be a disagreement set where each term in each disagreement pair in W is a normal form CTT term over $\mathcal{S} - \{\Pi\}$. If $\mathcal{T}_E W$ is a sound and complete set of E-unifiers for the disagreement set W, then $\mathcal{T}_E$ has the Logical Soundness and Logical Completeness properties.*

Proof: There is no loss of generality if we assume that for every $\langle p, s \rangle \in W$ that $p = s$ is a literal. If this does not hold then there are three cases: p and s are negative literals, or one of them is a negative literal and the other is a positive literal, or both of them are positive literals. In the first case, suppose that p has the form $\neg p'$ and s has the form $\neg s'$. The generalization depends on showing that $\mathcal{T}_E(W - \{\langle p, s \rangle\} \cup \{\langle p', s' \rangle\})$ is the same as $\mathcal{T}_E W$, and that $\models_\sim p'\theta = s'\theta$ if and only if $\models_\sim p\theta = s\theta$ where θ is a substitution. Both of these lemmas can be proved easily.

In the second case $\mathcal{T}_E W = \emptyset$, which also occurs in the third case when just one of the literals is an equation because by the fifth assumption of Remark 4.17 the matrix of an equation in E is a literal.

If p has the form $p_1 = s_1$ and s has the form $p_2 = s_2$ then similarly $\mathcal{T}_E(W - \{\langle p, s \rangle\} \cup \{\langle p_1, p_2 \rangle, \langle s_1, s_2 \rangle\})$ is the same as $\mathcal{T}_E W$. We also have that $\models_\sim p_1\theta = p_2\theta$ and $\models_\sim s_1\theta = s_2\theta$ if and only if $\models_\sim (p_1 = s_1)\theta = (p_2 = s_2)\theta$ where θ is a substitution.

We first show that $\mathcal{T}_E W$ has the Logical Soundness property. Let $E = \{q_i = r_i \mid i \in I\}$ and $\mathcal{R} = \{q_i \leftarrow r_i \mid i \in I\}$. Suppose $\sigma \in \mathcal{T}_E W$ and $\langle p, s \rangle \in W$. By Definition 4.12 of higher-order E-unifiability, we have $p\sigma \xleftrightarrow{*}_E s\sigma$. From the seventh assumption of Remark 4.17 we know that $\mathcal{R}$ is confluent, so that $p\sigma \downarrow_{\mathcal{R}} s\sigma$ by Definition 4.9. By Theorem 4.11, we have $E \vdash p\sigma = s\sigma$.

Suppose that $\sigma \leq_{\mathcal{F}(W)} \theta$, and μ is a substitution such that $\sigma\mu =_{\mathcal{F}(W)} \theta$, where μ has the form $\{\langle y_i, s_i \rangle \mid 0 \leq i \leq m\}$. From $E \vdash p\sigma = s\sigma$ we can derive $E \vdash p\theta = s\theta$, by m applications of the Abstraction Rule to form $E \vdash \lambda y_1. \cdots. \lambda y_m.p\sigma = \lambda y_1. \cdots. \lambda y_m.s\sigma$. By applying the Congruence Rule m times, we can then form

$$E \vdash (\cdots (\lambda y_1. \cdots. \lambda y_m.p\sigma \; s_1) \cdots s_m) = (\cdots (\lambda y_1. \cdots. \lambda y_m.s\sigma \; s_1) \cdots s_m)$$

which after repeated applications of the β-Reduction Rule yields $E \vdash p\theta = s\theta$. From Theorem 4.20, we have $\models_\sim p\theta = s\theta$, as required.

We now show that $\mathcal{T}_E W$ has the Logical Completeness property. We have $\models_\sim p\theta = s\theta$ for every $\langle p, s \rangle \in W$, so that by Theorem 4.20 we have $E \vdash p\theta = s\theta$. By the seventh assumption of Remark 4.17 and Theorem 4.11 it follows that $p\theta \downarrow_R s\theta$, so that $p\theta \xleftrightarrow{*}_E s\theta$. Hence, $\theta \in \mathcal{U}_E W$ by Definition 4.14, and the result follows from the Completeness part of Definition 4.22 of sound and complete set of E-unifiers. $\square$

Pure third-order equational matching is a special case of higher-order equational unification. We now consider its decidability.

4.1.3   Third-Order Equational Matching

First-order equational matching with constant symbols is undecidable [22, 85], but the pure third-order case does not seem to have been considered before. We now show that pure third-order equational matching is undecidable.

Hilbert's Tenth Problem [89] is to find an algorithm to determine if a polynomial

$$P(x_1, \ldots, x_n) = 0$$

has a solution in integers. This is known to be impossible because whether there is a solution to such a diophantine equation is recursively undecidable [132].

The problem of determining whether a diophantine equation has a solution in non-negative integers is also recursively undecidable. This follows from the observation that if the problem were decidable for non-negative integers, it would be decidable for integers by finding a non-negative integer solution to one of the equations $P(x_1, \ldots, x_n) = 0, P(-x_1, \ldots, x_n) = 0, \ldots, P(-x_1, \ldots, -x_n) = 0$ of which there are 2^n [41]. We show that third-order equational matching is undecidable by a reduction from the non-negative integer solution form of Hilbert's Tenth Problem.

Pure third-order equational matching is a higher-order equational unification problem in which terms do not contain constant symbols, the order of free variables is at most three, and at most one term in each disagreement pair can contain free variables.

Without loss of generality, we restrict attention to equations of the form

$$\exists x_1 \cdots x_n (p(x_1, \ldots, x_n) = q(x_1, \ldots, x_n)) \tag{4.1}$$

where $p(x_1, \ldots, x_n)$ and $q(x_1, \ldots, x_n)$ are polynomials with coefficients which are non-negative integers, and whose variables $x_1, \ldots, x_n$ range over non-negative integers.

The equation can be reduced to a pure third-order equational matching problem.

Definition 4.24 A non-negative integer constant, a numerical variable, $\times$, and $+$ are λ-definable (Definition 3.19) as follows:

- A coefficient or constant m is represented by the simply typed Church numeral
  $\overline{m} = \lambda xy. \underbrace{x(x(\cdots x(y)\cdots))}_{m}$ with type restricted to $N = ((\iota \to \iota), \iota \to \iota)$.

- A variable x is represented by the term $\overline{x}$ which is a variable with type N.

- Multiplication of terms of type N is represented by

$$\overline{\times} = \lambda xyz.x(y(z))$$

with type $(N, N \to N)$, where $\tau(z) = (\iota \to \iota)$.

- Addition of terms of type N is represented by

$$\mp = \lambda xyzt.x(z, y(z, t))$$

of type $(N, N \to N)$, where $\tau(z) = (\iota \to \iota)$ and $\tau(t) = \iota$.

Using these representations, the polynomials p and q can be encoded uniquely up to α-conversion as pure simply typed λ-terms, $\overline{p}$, and $\overline{q}$ in $\beta\overline{\eta}$-normal form, respectively. The matching problem is the following disagreement set.

$$\{\langle \lambda e.e(\overline{p}, \overline{q}), \ \lambda e.e(\lambda xy.y, \lambda xy.y) \rangle\} \tag{4.2}$$

where $\tau(e) = (N, N \to \iota)$.
  The equality theory E is

$$\{\lambda efg.e(\lambda xy.f(\lambda z.x(z), x(y)), \lambda xy.g(\lambda z.x(z), x(y)))$$
$$= \lambda efg.e(\lambda xy.f(\lambda z.x(z), y), \lambda xy.g(\lambda z.x(z), y))\}$$

where $\tau(f) = N$ and $\tau(g) = N$.
  The equation states that two positive integers are equal if and only if their predecessors are equal. We have the following result.

Theorem 4.25 *Pure third-order equational matching is undecidable.*

Proof: Suppose that equation 4.1 has a solution in non-negative integers. By substituting the encodings of these values for the encodings of $x_1, \ldots, x_n$ in equation 4.2 and then successively rewriting with equation 4.3, the encoding of the evaluations of p and q will be decremented simultaneously to the encodings of zero.
  If a substitution θ is a solution of the matching equation 4.2, then $\mathcal{F}(\lambda e.e(\overline{p}, \overline{q})\theta) = \emptyset$. Statman [183] has shown that the only closed pure λ-terms of type N are the simply typed Church numerals. All of the free variables in equation 4.2 have type N. Therefore, θ replaces each of these variables by simply typed Church numerals, and they are the encodings of a solution to equation 4.1. $\square$

Theorem 4.25 implies that third- and higher orders of equational matching are undecidable, and that higher-order equational unification is undecidable.
  We now consider higher-order equational unification. The assumptions of Remark 4.17 no longer apply, except that substitutions are $\beta\overline{\eta}$-normalized substitutions.

4.2 Higher-Order Unification

The higher-order unification procedure we consider is a version of G.P. Huet's [97] whose procedure is based on that by D.C. Jensen and T. Pietrzykowski [106].

4.2.1   Higher-Order Unifiers

The definitions of unifiers are based on those of Huet [98].

Definition 4.26 A substitution γ is a *higher-order unifier* of the disagreement set

$$W = \{\langle t_1, s_1 \rangle, \ldots, \langle t_n, s_n \rangle\}$$

if and only if $t_i\gamma =_{\beta\overline{\eta}} s_i\gamma$ for $1 \leq i \leq n$. The set of all such unifiers is denoted by $\mathcal{U}W$.

Definition 4.27 A substitution γ is a *semi-unifier* or *matcher* of the disagreement set

$$W = \{\langle t_1, s_1 \rangle, \ldots, \langle t_n, s_n \rangle\}$$

if and only if $t_i\gamma =_{\beta\overline{\eta}} s_i$ for $1 \leq i \leq n$. The set of all such semi-unifiers is denoted by $\mathcal{M}W$.

Consider the substitution ζ which is defined as follows.

Definition 4.28 For every type symbol $\alpha = (\alpha_1, \ldots, \alpha_{n-1} \to \alpha_n)$ where $\alpha_n \in T_0$ and $n \geq 1$, the term $\hat{\imath}_\alpha$ is as $\lambda w_1 \ldots w_{n-1}.w_n$ where the w_i are distinct variables and $\tau(w_i) = \alpha_i$ for $1 \leq i \leq n$. The substitution ζ is then defined as $\{\langle x, \hat{\imath}_{\tau(x)} \rangle | x \in \mathcal{X}\}$.

Definition 4.29 A substitution γ is a *pre-unifier* of the disagreement set

$$W = \{\langle t_1, s_1 \rangle, \ldots, \langle t_n, s_n \rangle\}$$

if and only if $t_i\gamma\zeta =_{\beta\overline{\eta}} s_i\gamma\zeta$ for $1 \leq i \leq n$. The set of all such pre-unifiers is denoted by $\mathcal{P}W$.

Definition 4.30 Let Γ and Λ be sets of substitutions,

$$W = \{\langle t_1, s_1 \rangle, \ldots, \langle t_n, s_n \rangle\}$$

be a disagreement set, $L = \cup_{1 \leq i \leq n}(\mathcal{F}(t_i) \cup \mathcal{F}(s_i))$, and V be a set of variables such that $L \subset V$. Consider the following four properties:

1. *Soundness.* $\Gamma \subseteq \Lambda$.

2. *Completeness.* $\forall \rho \in \Lambda : \exists \gamma \in \Gamma : \rho \leq_V \gamma$.

3. *Minimality.* $\forall \gamma_1, \gamma_2 \in \Gamma : (\gamma_1 \neq \gamma_2) \Rightarrow \gamma_1 \not\leq_L \gamma_2$.

4. *Independence.* $\forall \gamma_1, \gamma_2 \in \Gamma : (\gamma_1 \neq \gamma_2) \Rightarrow \neg \exists \eta \eta' : \gamma_1 \eta =_L \gamma_2 \eta'$.

Definition 4.31 Using the four properties above, we can classify certain sets of substitutions.

- If $\Lambda = \mathcal{U}W$ and Γ satisfies properties 1, 2, and 3, then Γ is a *complete set of minimal unifiers (CSMU)* of W on V.

- If $\Lambda = \mathcal{M}W$ and Γ satisfies properties 1, 2, and 3, then Γ is a *complete set of minimal semi-unifiers (CSMS)* of W on V.

- If $\Lambda = \mathcal{P}W$ and $\Gamma = \{\theta\zeta | \theta \in \Theta\}$ satisfies properties 1,2, and 4, then Θ is a *complete set of independent pre-unifiers (CSIP)* of W on V.

4.2.2 Higher-Order Pre-Unification Procedure

The Soundness and Completeness properties of Definition 4.30 are equivalent to those of Definition 4.22 for higher-order equational unification when $E = \emptyset$, $\sim$ is the relation $=_{\beta\bar{\eta}}$, $\Gamma = \mathcal{T}_{\emptyset}W$, and $\Lambda = \mathcal{U}_{\emptyset}W$. Huet's higher-order pre-unification procedure [97] for the $\beta\bar{\eta}$-calculus is a procedure $\mathcal{T}_{\emptyset}$. It recursively enumerates a complete set of independent pre-unifiers, and so has the Soundness and Completeness properties of Definition 4.23.

The pre-unification procedure builds a tree each of whose nodes is a disagreement set. The root of the tree is initially the original disagreement set. Whenever a new node is added to the tree an algorithm called SIMPL is applied to the node. SIMPL either indicates that the node is not unifiable, or replaces it by a simplified disagreement set which has the same set of pre-unifiers.

SIMPL has three steps. In the first step, each disagreement pair

$$\langle \lambda u_1 \cdots u_n.@_1(t_1, \ldots, t_p), \lambda v_1 \cdots v_n.@_2(s_1, \ldots, s_q) \rangle$$

in the node is treated in turn. Each disagreement pair has this form because all terms are in $\beta\bar{\eta}$-normal form. If

$$@_1 \neq_{\beta\bar{\eta}} (\lambda v_1 \cdots v_n.@_2)(u_1, \ldots u_n)$$

then SIMPL indicates that the node is not unifiable. Otherwise, $p = q$, and the disagreement pair is replaced by p pairs of the form

$$\langle \lambda u_1 \cdots u_n.t_i, \lambda v_1 \cdots v_n.s_i \rangle$$

where $0 \leq i \leq p$, and the first step is repeated.

Terms are classified into two forms: flexible and rigid. If the head of a term is a free variable, then the term is a flexible, otherwise it is a rigid term. Disagreement pairs are either called flexible-flexible, flexible-rigid, rigid-flexible, or rigid-rigid, by using the respective classifications of the terms in the pair. In the second step of SIMPL, each rigid-flexible disagreement pair is transformed into a flexible-rigid pair by transposing its terms.

In the third step, if there exists a rigid-rigid disagreement pair in the node then SIMPL indicates that the node is not unifiable. Otherwise, SIMPL terminates.

Here is an example of the effects of SIMPL [97].

Example 4.32 Applying SIMPL to the node

$$\{\langle A(\lambda u.B(x, u), C), A(\lambda v.B(y, v), f(C)) \rangle\}$$

produces the node

$$\{\langle \lambda u.x, \lambda v.y \rangle, \langle f(C), C \rangle\}.$$

$\bigcirc$

The algorithm for adding nodes to the tree is called MATCH. It has two rules: imitation and projection, which apply a substitution to a node to produce a descendant

node. To ensure that a complete set of independent pre-unifiers is enumerated, all new
free variables in a substitution generated by applying MATCH to a node must be unique,
or different from all free variables in substitutions used in forming the branch from the
root of the tree to that node. MATCH is only applied to a node after SIMPL has been
applied to it, and when SIMPL has not indicated that the node is not unifiable.

Suppose that SIMPL terminates without indicating that the node it was applied to
is not unifiable. If the node is the empty set, or each disagreement pair in the node is
flexible-flexible, then the node is unifiable. The substitution ζ of Definition 4.28 unifies
the flexible-flexible pairs.

However, if there is a flexible-rigid disagreement pair of the form

$$\langle \lambda u_1 \ldots u_n . f(t_1, \ldots, t_p), \lambda v_1 \ldots v_n . B(F_1, \ldots, F_q) \rangle$$

where $\tau(f) = (\alpha_1, \ldots, \alpha_p \to \beta)$ the MATCH algorithm is invoked. It has two rules:
imitation, and projection.

There can be at most one substitution produced by imitation.

Definition 4.33 An *imitation substitution* has the form

$$\langle f, \ \lambda w_1 \ldots w_p . B(\lambda \overline{y_1} . h_1(w_1, \ldots, w_p, \overline{y_1}), \ldots, \lambda \overline{y_q} . h_q(w_1, \ldots, w_p, \overline{y_q})) \rangle$$

where

- B is a constant symbol,

- $\tau(w_i) = \alpha_i$ for $1 \leq i \leq p$,

- the h_j are distinct free variables called *introduced variables* which satisfy the condition for complete matching trees above and have types $(\alpha_1, \ldots, \alpha_p \to \tau(F_j))$ for
  $1 \leq j \leq q$,

- and $\overline{y_j}$ is a finite sequence of variables such that

$$\lambda \overline{y_j} . h_j(w_1, \ldots, w_p, \overline{y_j})$$

  is in $\beta \overline{\eta}$-normal form where $1 \leq j \leq q$.

There can also be at most p substitutions produced by projection.

Definition 4.34 A *projection substitution* has the form

$$\{ \langle f, \ \lambda w_1 \cdots w_p . w_i (\lambda \overline{y_1} . h_1(w_1, \ldots, w_p, \overline{y_1}), \ldots, \lambda \overline{y_k} . h_k(w_1, \ldots, w_p, \overline{y_k})) \rangle \}.$$

for each $i : 1 \leq i \leq p$ where

- $\tau(f) = (\alpha_1, \ldots, \alpha_p \to \beta)$,

- $\beta \in T_o$,

- $\alpha_i = (\beta_1, \ldots, \beta_k \to \beta)$,

- $\tau(w_j) = \alpha_j$, for $1 \leq j \leq p$,

- $\tau(h_l) = (\alpha_1, \ldots, \alpha_p \to \beta_l)$ where $1 \leq l \leq k$, and h_l are distinct free variables called *introduced variables* which satisfy the condition for complete matching trees above, and

- $\overline{y_l}$ is a finite sequence of variables such that $\lambda \overline{y_l}.h_l(w_1, \ldots, w_p, \overline{y_l})$ is in $\beta\overline{\eta}$-normal form where $1 \leq l \leq k$.

After MATCH has been applied to a node, it can have at most $p+1$ direct descendant nodes, where each such node is the result of applying the imitation substitution or one of the projection substitution to all terms in the parent node.

Here is an example of the effects of MATCH [97].

Example 4.35 Applying MATCH to the node

$$\{\langle f(f(x)), \, A(A(B)) \rangle\}$$

produces the nodes $\{\langle x, \, B \rangle\}$, $\{\langle f, \, \lambda u.A(h(u)) \rangle\}$, and $\{\langle x, \, A(A(B)) \rangle\}$. $\bigcirc$

A leaf of the tree is either the empty set, a node just containing flexible-flexible disagreement pairs, or a node which SIMPL has indicated is not unifiable. In the first two cases, a pre-unifier $\theta_1 \cdots \theta_k$ of the root of the tree is formed by composing the substitutions $\theta_1, \theta_2, \ldots, \theta_k$ generated by applications of MATCH in forming the branch of the tree containing the leaf. The collection of all such pre-unifiers is a complete set of independent pre-unifiers for the root of the tree [97].

4.2.3 Heuristics and Implementations

Huet [97] gives four heuristics for higher-order unification procedures:

Eventuality. Each instance of a flexible-rigid pair should be selected for MATCH after a finite number of applications of MATCH. Otherwise nonunifiability may not be detected.

Subsumption. A branch in the matching tree can be truncated without loss of completeness if the most recently generated node is an α-variant of an earlier node in the branch.

Collapsing. If $\langle x, E \rangle$ occurs in a node of the matching tree and $x \notin \mathcal{F}(E)$, then $\{\langle x, E \rangle\}$ is a most general unifier of x and E. This implies that SIMPL can be modified so that such a disagreement pair $\langle x, E \rangle$ is deleted from a node and the substitution $\{\langle x, E \rangle\}$ is applied to the node.

Rigid-Path Occurs Check. A *rigid path* for x in E is defined as a sequence of terms $E = E_1, E_2, \ldots, E_n, E_{n+1}, (n \geq 1)$ which satisfies the following conditions:

- $\forall i : (1 \leq i \leq n) \ E_{i+1}$ is an argument of E_i.

- $\forall i : (1 \le i \le n) \exists j : (1 \le j \le i)$ the head of E_i is a constant or a variable in the binder of some E_j.

- the head of E_{n+1} is an occurrence of x free in E.

SIMPL can be modified to detect nonunifiability when either E has an empty binder and there exists a rigid path for x in E, or if there exists a rigid path for x in E and its last element E_{n+1} has no arguments. The occurs check for first-order unification is a special case.

The theorem prover *TPS* [136] also allows pre-unification without the $\bar{\eta}$-rule. TPS uses the collapsing and rigid-path occurs check heuristics and it does not include a disagreement pair in a node if it is an α-variant of another disagreement pair in that node. A heuristic used to select the next disagreement pair for MATCH chooses the disagreement pair which would result in the minimum number of direct descendant nodes.

Another heuristic used in TPS, which is an extension of the subsumption heuristic, is to truncate a branch in a matching tree when a proper subset of the most recently generated node is an α-variant of an earlier node in the branch. A subtree of the matching tree is pruned if the most recently generated node is an α-variant of a proper subset of the root of the subtree. The most recently generated node is possibly retained in this case.

The theorem prover *Isabelle* [149] uses a version of higher-order pre-unification which assumes the $\bar{\eta}$-rule. The collapsing and rigid-path occurs check heuristics are incorporated. Pairs of flexible terms are reduced and kept as constraints on future unification problems in the same proof.

The implementation of the logic programming language $\lambda Prolog$ also assumes the $\bar{\eta}$--rule for higher-order unification [143]. It incorporates a generalization of the collapsing heuristic. A most general unifier for the flexible-rigid disagreement pair $\langle F_1, F \rangle$ where the β-normal form of F_1 is $\lambda y_1 \ldots y_n.x(y_{p_1}, \ldots, y_{p_n})$ and $p_1, \ldots, p_n$ is the effect of a permutation on $1, \ldots, n$, is the substitution

$$\sigma = \{\langle x, \ \lambda y_{p_1} \ldots y_{p_n}.F(y_1, \ldots, y_n) \rangle\}$$

provided none of the variables $y_1, \ldots, y_n$ or x occurs free in F. The pair $\langle F_1, F \rangle$ is deleted by SIMPL and σ is applied to the node.

C. Elliott and F. Pfenning [51] describe a higher-order program derivation method following Huet and Lang's [103] second-order method. The $\bar{\eta}$-rule is assumed. They derive a higher-order unification procedure from its specification. An heuristic used with the derived procedure factors nodes which are α-variants and which occur on separate branches of the matching tree, so that the matching tree is transformed to a matching directed acyclic graph. Disagreement sets are partitioned into subsets which do not share any free variables. These subsets can be solved independently and their solutions composed to form solutions to the initial disagreement set. They state that such partitioning can often reduce an exponentially large matching tree to a matching directed acyclic graph which is quadratic in the size of the original disagreement set.

Snyder and Gallier [67, 182] present sound and complete higher-order unification procedures using a generalization of the elementary transformations for first-order unification discussed by Martelli and Montanari [130]. They give a procedure where the $\bar{\eta}$-rule is assumed, and one where it is not assumed. They show that the heuristic of *eager variable elimination*, in which the collapsing heuristic is always applied as soon as possible, is sound and complete.

4.2.4   Undecidability Results

Statman [184] has shown that the set of all decidable unification problems is polynomial time decidable. The proof of this result is not a constructive one and it only applies to the $\beta\bar{\eta}$-calculus. By classifying unification problems by their type, it can be shown that there are decidable unification problems of arbitrarily high order [184].

   An example of this occurs when every free variable f in the terms in $\beta\bar{\eta}$-normal form in a disagreement set occurs in a subterm of the form $f(x_1, \ldots, x_n)$ where the x_i are distinct bound variables [135]. The complexity of solving a unification problem whose terms have this form is linear in space and time [162].

   In the general case, third- and second-order unification problems are undecidable. This implies that all unifiability and pre-unifiability problems of higher orders are also undecidable. This is not a reason for avoiding higher order unification; Isabelle [151], TPS [136], and λProlog [139] use it intensively and show in practice that most time is spent searching for proofs rather than for unifiers.

   We now consider the reductions from Post's Correspondence Problem, and Hilbert's Tenth Problem which were used in the proofs of these results.

Third-Order Unification

G.P. Huet [96] has shown that the problem of whether there exists a unifier for two third-order (or higher order) terms is recursively undecidable[1] by reducing Post's Correspondence Problem[2] to it.

   The reduction maps any instance of Post's Correspondence Problem

$$\{(x_i, y_i) | 1 \leq i \leq n\}$$

where x_i and y_i are strings over the alphabet $\Sigma = \{U, V\}$ for $1 \leq i \leq n$, to the third-order unification problem for the two terms:

$$\lambda uvh.h(f(\tilde{x}_1, \ldots, \tilde{x}_n), f(\lambda w.u(w), \ldots, \lambda w.u(w)))$$

and

$$\lambda uvh.h(f(\tilde{y}_1, \ldots, \tilde{y}_n), u(g(\lambda w.u(w))))$$

where every word $\tilde{z} \in \Sigma^*$ is associated with a term according to the rules: $\tilde{\epsilon} = \lambda t.t$, $\widetilde{Uz} = \lambda t.u(\tilde{z}(t))$, and $\widetilde{Vz} = \lambda t.v(\tilde{z}(t))$. The types of the variables are

$$\tau(u) \;\; = \;\; \tau(v) = \tau(\tilde{x}_i) = \tau(\tilde{y}_i) = (\iota \rightarrow \iota), \;\; 1 \leq i \leq n$$

---

[1]Huet notes that this was also shown in C.L. Lucchesi, The Undecidability of the Unification Problem for Third-Order Languages, Report CSRR 2059, Department of Applied Analysis and Computer Science, University of Waterloo, Waterloo, Ontario, 1972.

[2]This problem originally appeared in: E. Post, A Variant of a Recursively Unsolvable Problem, *Bull. AMS* **52** (1946) 264–268, and it is discussed in, for example, Hopcroft and Ullman [94].

$$\begin{aligned}
\tau(h) &= (\iota, \iota \to \iota) \\
\tau(f) &= \underbrace{((\iota \to \iota), \ldots, (\iota \to \iota)}_{n} \to \iota), \ n \geq 1 \\
\tau(w) &= \tau(t) = \iota \\
\tau(g) &= ((\iota \to \iota) \to \iota).
\end{aligned}$$

If $i_1, \ldots, i_p, (p \geq 1)$ is a solution to the instance of Post's Correspondence Problem (i.e. if $x_{i_1} \cdots x_{i_p} = y_{i_1} \cdots y_{i_p}$), then

$$\{\langle f, \ \lambda w_1 \ldots w_n.w_{i_1}(w_{i_2}(\cdots w_{i_p}(s)\cdots)))\rangle, \langle g, \ \lambda u.\underbrace{u(\cdots u}_{p-1}(s)\cdots))\rangle\}$$

where $\tau(w_i) = (\iota \to \iota)$ for $1 \leq i \leq n$ is a unifier of the two terms. Huet also shows that every solution to the unification problem implies a solution to the Post's Correspondence Problem.

Second-Order Unification

W. Goldfarb [76] subsequently showed that the unification of second-order terms is also recursively undecidable by a reduction from Hilbert's Tenth Problem (the general solution of a finite set of Diophantine equations), any instance of which can be written as a finite set of equations of the forms $x_i \cdot x_j = x_k$, $x_i + x_j = x_k$, and $x_i = C_j$ where the x are numerical variables, and the C_j are numerical constants.

Terms are constructed in the proof to represent numerical constants, and disagreement pairs are constructed to represent equations in any instance of Hilbert's Tenth Problem. If C denotes a natural number $c \geq 0$, it is represented by the term $\bar{c}A$, where $\bar{c}$ is the curried typed Church numeral

$$(\lambda ty. \underbrace{t(\cdots t}_{c}(y)\cdots)\lambda x.G(A, x))$$

and $\tau(A) = \tau(x) = \tau(y) = \iota$, $\tau(G) = (\iota, \iota \to \iota)$, and $\tau(\bar{c}) = \tau(t) = (\iota \to \iota)$. For example, $\bar{0}A = A$ and $\bar{2}A = G(A, G(A, A))$. The equation $x_i = C_j$ where x_i is a numerical variable is represented by the pair of terms $\langle f_i(A), \overline{c_j}A\rangle$ where $\tau(f_i) = \iota$.

An equation $x_i + x_j = x_k$ is represented by the pair of terms $\langle f_i(f_j(A)), f_k(A)\rangle$. The substitution

$$\{\langle f_i, \ \lambda w_1.\bar{n}w_1\rangle, \langle f_j, \ \lambda w_1.\bar{m}w_1\rangle, \langle f_k, \ \lambda w_1.\bar{p}w_1\rangle\}$$

where $\tau(w_1) = \iota$ is a unifier for the pair of terms if and only if $p = m + n$.

Similarly, an equation $x_i \cdot x_j = x_k$ is represented by the set with disagreement pairs

$$\langle h_l(A, B, G(G(f_k(A), f_j(B)), A)), G(G(A, B), h_l(f_i(A), G(A, B), A))\rangle,$$
$$\langle h_l(B, A, G(G(f_k(B), f_j(A)), A)), G(G(B, A), h_l(f_i(B), G(A, A), A))\rangle$$

where $\tau(h_l) = (\iota, \iota, \iota \to \iota)$ and $l = 2^i 3^j 5^k$. The substitution

$$\{\langle f_i, \ \lambda w_1.\bar{m}w_1\rangle, \langle f_j, \ \lambda w_1.\bar{n}w_1\rangle, \langle f_k, \ \lambda w_1.\bar{p}w_1\rangle, \langle h_l, \ \lambda w_1 w_2 w_3.u\rangle\}$$

where $u = w_3$ if $n = 0$, and if $n > 0$ then u is

$$G(G(w_1, w_2), G(G(\overline{m.1}w_1, \overline{1}w_2), .., G(G(\overline{m.(n-1)}w_1, \overline{n-1}w_2), w_3) \cdots))$$

and $\tau(w_2) = \tau(w_3) = \iota$, is a unifier for the disagreement set if and only if $p = m \cdot n$.

Farmer [55] has refined this result by showing that there is a natural number n such that the unification problem is undecidable for all second-order languages which contain a binary function constant and at least n function variables whose type symbols are not elementary type symbols. This result has an application to the problem of the decidability of k-provability for first-order axiom schemata and rules of inference called Parikh systems [56]. It was refined further by Narendran [144] to the monadic case. The reduction used is discussed in Section 4.2.4 below.

It has also been shown by Amiot that the second-order predicate unification problem is undecidable by reducing the second-order unification problem to it [2]. The reduction linearly encodes second-order terms into systems of pairs of second-order atomic formulas which have individual and predicate variables, individual and function constants, and a monadic predicate constant only.

Although second-order unification and second-order predicate unification are recursively undecidable, second-order matching and first-order unification [103, 166] are decidable. These proofs are based on lexicographic orderings of sets of terms produced after each iteration of the matching and unification algorithms.

Third-Order Monadic Unification

Narendran [144] has shown that third-order monadic unification is undecidable by a reduction from Hilbert's Tenth Problem. The reduction is a variant of Goldfarb's [76], which was discussed in Section 4.2.4. This undecidabilty result refines that of third-order unification [96] of Section 4.2.4.

The reduction for addition is the same as that used by Goldfarb [76]. The numerals are encoded as follows:

$$\overline{0} = \lambda x.x$$
$$\overline{1} = \lambda x.S(x)$$
$$\vdots$$
$$\overline{n+1} = \lambda x.S(\overline{n}(x))$$

Each encoded numeral has type $(\alpha \to \alpha)$ where $\alpha \in T_0$.

It can be shown that multiplication $r = p * q$ can be reduced to the disagreement set

$$\{\langle f(\lambda x.x), C\rangle, \langle f(S), \overline{p}(C)\rangle, \langle f(\overline{q}), \overline{r}(C)\rangle\}$$

where f is a third-order monadic function symbol, and $\tau(f) = ((\alpha \to \alpha) \to \alpha)$. This disagreement set has a solution if and only if $r = p * q$.

4.3   Higher-Order Matching

We consider approaches for resolving the open problem of the decidability of matching for the typed λ-calculus where the $\overline{\eta}$-rule of conversion is assumed[3]

Although second-order and third-order matching are decidable [48, 103], the decidability of the general problem is unknown [98].

Huet and Lang [103] define the matching problem as follows:

> Let t and t' be two terms of the same type. The term t matches t' if and only if there exists a substitution γ such that $t' = \gamma t$.

Higher-order matching is another special case of higher-order equational unification. They also note that:

> We assume that t' does not contain free variables. If this is not the case, just "freeze" the free variables x_i of t' into new constants X_i when matching t to t', and do the inverse transformation in [the set of matchers].

Higher-order matching with freezing is a step in Definition 4.4 of the higher-order rewrite relation which was used to define higher-order equational unification. The substitution π in Definition 4.4 is a higher-order matching substitution found by freezing free variables in $matrix(p/i)$. If higher-order matching is decidable, then the applicability of a higher-order rewrite rule is decidable.

The correctness of this method of treating free variables was presented and proved by Huet [98] (Lemma 3.16), where $\overline{\eta}$-conversion is not assumed. The next section is my translation of part of this work.

4.3.1   Freezing Lemma

It is easy to reduce the problem of semi-unification to a special case of unification with one closed term, by "freezing" the variables of t'. More precisely, given $\mathcal{F}(t') = \{x_1, \ldots, x_k\}$, we introduce k new constant symbols $X_1, \ldots, X_k$ such that $\tau(x_i) = \tau(X_i)$ for $1 \leq i \leq k$, and we consider $\xi = \{\langle x_i, X_i \rangle \mid 1 \leq i \leq k\}$. Such a substitution has a natural inverse. In other words, for all terms e formed from $\mathcal{C}' = \mathcal{C} \cup \{X_1, \ldots, X_k\}$ with $\mathcal{F}(t) \cap \mathcal{F}(t') = \emptyset$, there is a unique term e' formed from $\mathcal{C}$, and such that $\xi e' = e$. Effectively, we can define such an e' along with ξ^{-1}, by:

$$\xi^{-1}[\lambda u_1 \cdots u_n.@(e_1, \ldots, e_p)] = \lambda u_1 \cdots u_n.@'(\xi^{-1}[e_1], \ldots, \xi^{-1}[e_p])$$

where

$$@' = \begin{cases} @ & \text{if } @ \in V \cup \mathcal{C} \\ x_i & \text{if } @ = X_i, 1 \leq i \leq k \end{cases}$$

The square brackets are used to emphasize that ξ^{-1} is not a substitution. It is easy to show, by induction on e, that: $\xi \xi^{-1}[e] = e$ for all e such that $\mathcal{F}(t) \cap \mathcal{F}(t') = \emptyset$, and $\xi^{-1}[\xi e] = e$ for all e formed from $\mathcal{C}$.

We now show how it is possible to form a CSMS of t to t' from a CSIP of ξt and $\xi t'$.

---

[3]I presented the results of this Section, and Section 4.4 at INRIA, Rocquencourt in January 1990, and at the University of Cambridge Computer Laboratory in February 1990.

Lemma 4.36 *Let t and t' be two terms of the same type, $V = \mathcal{F}(t) - \mathcal{F}(t')$, and $L = \mathcal{F}(t) \cup \mathcal{F}(t')$. Let Γ be a CSIP of ξt and $\xi t'$ on V such that $\forall \gamma \in \Gamma : I(\gamma) \cap \mathcal{F}(t') = \emptyset$. For all $\gamma \in \Gamma$, define $\gamma' = \{\langle x, \xi^{-1}[\gamma x]\rangle \mid x \in V\}$. Then $\Gamma' = \{\gamma' \mid \gamma \in \Gamma\}$ is a CSMS of t to t' on L.*[4]

Example. Given $t = f(A)$ and $t' = g(A)$ where $\tau(A) = \alpha$ and $\tau(f) = \tau(g) = (\alpha \to \alpha)$, we have here that $V = \{f\}$, $L = \{f, g\}$, and $\xi = \{\langle g, G\rangle\}$.

We can show that $\Gamma = \{\langle f, \lambda u.G(u)\rangle, \langle f, \lambda u.G(A)\rangle, \langle f, G\rangle\}$ is a CSIP of ξt and $\xi t'$ on V.

Thus, $\Gamma' = \{\langle f, \lambda u.g(u)\rangle, \langle f, \lambda u.g(A)\rangle, \langle f, g\rangle\}$ is a CSMS of t to t' on L. $\square$

Remark. In this example we show that the independence condition of Γ, even if it implies the minimality condition of Γ', does not also imply an independence condition for Γ'.

We have, for example,

$$\eta\{\langle f, \lambda u.g(u)\rangle\} = \eta\{\langle f, \lambda u.g(A)\rangle\},$$

with $\eta = \{\langle g, \lambda u.g(A)\rangle\}$. We cannot hope to find a complete set of independent semi-unifiers when $\mathcal{F}(t') \neq \emptyset$, and this holds for restrictions to second-order problems.

Notes.

1. In practice, there is no need to bring in ξ explicitly. It suffices to "freeze" the occurrences of free variables in $\mathcal{F}(t')$, in the same way that SIMPL and MATCH treat constant symbols. Clearly the set $\Gamma(A)$ so obtained will immediately be $\Gamma(A)'$.

2. We conjecture that the unifiability of t and t' is decidable when $\mathcal{F}(t') = \emptyset$. This result naturally entails the decidability of semi-unification.

4.4 Decidability of Matching

Huet [98] conjectures that "this problem is decidable, but the proof is probably hard". In a later note (June 1985) [99], Huet states "Apparently, the decidability of matching in ω-order logic is still an open problem."

4.4.1 Examples of Nontermination

Suppose we have a definition of the size of a term, and lexicographically order disagreement pairs using this measure. If the original disagreement set is $\{\langle \mathbf{lhs}, \mathbf{rhs}\rangle\}$, then the number of matching substitutions is not in general exponentially bounded by $size(\mathbf{lhs})$.

Example 4.37 M. Zaionc [203] shows that the higher-order matching problem

$$\{\langle g(\lambda x.x), B(A)\rangle\}$$

---

[4]The proof shows that Γ' has the properties of soundness, completeness, and minimality.

where $\tau(g) = ((\iota \to \iota) \to \iota)$, $\tau(x) = \tau(A) = \iota$, and $\tau(B) = (\iota \to \iota)$ has solution

$$\{\langle g, \ \lambda u. \underbrace{u(\cdots u}_{m}(B(\underbrace{u(\cdots u}_{n}(A)\cdots)))\cdots)\rangle \mid m, n \geq 0\}.$$

The cardinality of this set of match substitutions is ω, which is not bounded by an exponential function of $size(g(\lambda x.x))$. $\bigcirc$

The pair $\langle size(\mathbf{lhs}), size(\mathbf{rhs}) \rangle$ also does not in general decrease lexicographically. We define $size(t)$ to be the number of times the symbol λ occurs in the $\beta\bar\eta$-normal form of the term t.

Example 4.38 Consider the matching problem

$$D_0 = \{\langle \lambda uv.f(\lambda xy.x(y)), \ \lambda uv.A(u,v)\rangle\}$$

where $\tau(f) = (((o \to o), o \to o) \to o)$, $\tau(x) = (o \to o)$, and $\tau(y) = o$. We have $size(\lambda uv.f(\lambda xy.x(y))) = 2$. If the projection

$$\pi_0 = \{\langle f, \ \lambda w_1.w_1(\lambda w_2.h_1(w_1, w_2), h_2(w_1))\rangle\}$$

is applied, we obtain the disagreement pair

$$D_1 = \{\langle \lambda uv.h_1(\lambda xy.x(y), h_2(\lambda xy.x(y))), \ \lambda uv.A(u,v)\rangle\}.$$

We now have $size(\lambda uv.h_1(\lambda xy.x(y), h_2(\lambda xy.x(y)))) = 3$. Using our size measure which seems "reasonable", $\langle size(\mathbf{lhs}), size(\mathbf{rhs}) \rangle$ has *increased* lexicographically from $\langle 2, 1\rangle$ to $\langle 3, 1\rangle$. If the projection

$$\pi_1 = \{\langle h_1, \ \lambda w_1 w_2.w_1(\lambda w_3.h_3(w_1, w_2, w_3), h_4(w_1, w_2))\rangle\}$$

is then applied to D_1, the flexible term in D_2 is

$$\lambda uv.h_3(\lambda xy.x(y), h_2(\lambda xy.x(y)), h_4(\lambda xy.x(y), h_2(\lambda xy.x(y))))$$

The disagreement pair D_2 has $\langle size(\mathbf{lhs}), size(\mathbf{rhs}) \rangle$ equal to $\langle 5, 1\rangle$. It is easy to verify that if this sequence of projections is continued by always projecting the first immediate subterm $\lambda xy.x(y)$ of the flexible term, D_i has $\langle size(\mathbf{lhs}), size(\mathbf{rhs}) \rangle$ equal to $\langle 2^i + 1, 1\rangle$. $\bigcirc$

4.4.2 Removing Constant Symbols

Statman [184] has shown that unification and matching problems involving constant symbols can be transformed into ones in the pure simply typed λ-calculus without loss of generality. Imitation substitutions are inapplicable for such problems.

Let $\{\langle t_i, s_i\rangle \mid 1 \leq i \leq m\}$ be a unification problem with a unifier

$$\{\langle x_j, r_j\rangle \mid 1 \leq j \leq k\}$$

where $\bigcup_{1 \leq i \leq n}(\mathcal{F}(t_i) \cup \mathcal{F}(s_i)) = \{x_1, \ldots, x_k\}$. Let $\{C_1, \ldots, C_n\}$ be constant symbols occurring in s_i and t_i where $1 \leq i \leq n$.

We now define a replacement of a constant symbol by a variable.

Definition 4.39 The *constant symbol replacement* of constant symbol C by a variable x in term t is

$$t\{(C, x)\} = (\cdots((t[i_1 \leftarrow x])[i_2 \leftarrow x])\cdots)[i_n \leftarrow x]$$

where $\{i_1, \ldots, i_n\} = \{i \in \mathcal{O}(t) \mid t/i = C\}$ and $\tau(x) = \tau(C)$.

Using such replacements, the unification problem can be transformed to the unification problem $\{\langle t_i^*, s_i^* \rangle \mid 1 \leq i \leq m\}$ without constant symbols, where t_i^* is the $\beta\overline{\eta}$-normal form of

$$\lambda y_1 \cdots y_n.(\lambda x_1 \cdots x_k.t_i'(h_1(y_1, \ldots, y_n), \ldots, h_k(y_1, \ldots, y_n)))$$

where t_i' is $(\cdots(t_i\{(C_1, y_1)\})\cdots)\{(C_n, y_n)\})$, $1 \leq i \leq m$, and h_j are new free variables of type $(\tau(y_1), \ldots, \tau(y_n) \rightarrow \tau(x_j))$ where $1 \leq j \leq k$.

A similar transformation is used to form the s_i^*:

$$\{\langle x_j, \lambda y_1 \cdots y_n.((\cdots(r_j\{(C_1, y_1)\})\cdots\{(C_n, y_n)\}))\rangle \mid 1 \leq j \leq k\}.$$

These transformations can be reversed. There is a bijection between unifiers of a unification problem with constant symbols, and unifiers of its transformed version without constant symbols [184].

Transforming a unification problem to one without constants can increase the order of the problem which can be seen from the types of the introduced variables h_j.

For example, the matching problem [97, 153] $\{\langle f(f(x)), A(A(B)) \rangle\}$ has matching substitutions

$$\mu_0 = \{\langle f, \lambda y.y \rangle, \langle x, A(A(B)) \rangle\}$$

$$\mu_1 = \{\langle f, \lambda u.A(u) \rangle, \langle x, B \rangle\}$$

and

$$\mu_2 = \{\langle f, \lambda u.A(A(B)) \rangle\}.$$

Applying the above transformation above gives the matching problem

$$\{\langle \lambda y_1 y_2.h_1(y_1, y_2, h_1(y_1, y_2, h_2(y_1, y_2))), \lambda y_1 y_2.y_1(y_1(y_2)) \rangle\}$$

because

$$f(f(x))^* \text{ is } \lambda y_1 y_2.(\lambda f x.f(f(x))(\lambda y_3.h_1(y_1, y_2, y_3), h_2(y_1, y_2)))$$

and

$$A(A(B))^* \text{ is } \lambda y_1 y_2.(\lambda f x.y_1(y_1(y_2))(\lambda y_3.h_1(y_1, y_2, y_3), h_2(y_1, y_2))).$$

The transformed problem has these respective matching substitutions:

$$\mu_0^* = \{\langle h_1, \lambda z_1 z_2 z_3.z_3 \rangle, \langle h_2, \lambda z_1 z_2.z_1(z_1(z_2)) \rangle\}$$

$$\mu_1^* = \{\langle h_1, \lambda z_1 z_2 z_3.z_1(z_3) \rangle, \langle h_2, \lambda z_1 z_2.z_2 \rangle\}$$

and

$$\mu_2^* = \{\langle h_1, \lambda z_1 z_2 z_3.z_1(z_1(z_2)) \rangle\}.$$

4.4.3 An Algorithm for Higher-Order Matching

We now present a terminating procedure for higher-order matching. Initially, we shall just consider higher-order matching of pure simply typed λ-calculus terms. If Huet's procedure for higher-order unification is used, imitation substitutions are unnecessary and we need only consider projection substitutions.

If higher-order matching is decidable, then it is decidable whether or not an interior node of the MATCH tree for a matching problem is the root of a subtree which does not contain a node labelled S. It is also decidable if the most recent application of the projection rule which led to that node is redundant for finding matching substitutions. Our algorithm for higher-order matching prevents applications of the projection rule which could be redundant in this way.

Example 4.40 Every application of the projection rule for the disagreement set

$$\{\langle \lambda u.f(\lambda yz.y(z), \lambda x.x), \lambda u.u \rangle\}$$

must be redundant because there is no matching substitution. $\bigcirc$

This leads to the following definition.

Definition 4.41 From Definition 4.34, a projection substitution π has the form

$$\{\langle f, \lambda w_1 \cdots w_p.w_i(\lambda \overline{y_1}.h_1(w_1, \ldots, w_p, \overline{y_1}), \ldots, \lambda \overline{y_k}.h_k(w_1, \ldots, w_p, \overline{y_k})) \rangle\}$$

where f is the head of a flexible term t in a pair in a disagreement set, $1 \le i \le p$ and t/i meets certain type conditions.

The term t/i is called the *projectile* of t for π.

Theorem 4.4 of Huet [97] as modified for the $\beta\overline{\eta}$-calculus shows that MATCH trees can be used to enumerate a complete set of minimal matching substitutions independently of which disagreement pair is chosen from a disagreement set. Consequently, without losing completeness each instance of the same disagreement pair on a descendant branch can be repeatedly selected until it can be decomposed by SIMPL.

Definition 4.42 A MATCH tree for a higher-order matching problem is an *iterated MATCH tree* if and only if the following condition holds for every node

$$M_0 = \{\langle s_1, t_1 \rangle, \ldots, \langle s_n, t_n \rangle\}$$

of the MATCH tree where $n \ge 1$. Suppose that there is a branch

$$M_0 \longrightarrow_{\pi_0} M_1 \longrightarrow_{\pi_1} \cdots \longrightarrow_{\pi_{k-1}} M_k \longrightarrow_{\pi_k} \cdots$$

where the π_i are projection substitutions formed using the projection rule and $k \ge 0$, and the pair $\langle s_l, t_l \rangle$ was selected from M_0. The selected pair in M_j is $\langle s_l \pi_0 \cdots \pi_{j-1}, t_l \rangle$ where $1 \le j < k$ and M_k is the first descendant node of M_0 on this branch where SIMPL can decompose $\langle s_l \pi_0 \cdots \pi_{k-1}, t_l \rangle$.

Example 4.43 If the pair

$$\langle \lambda uv.f(f(x, \lambda g.h(u, v(u, d(u)))), \lambda x.e(x)), \ \lambda uv.v(u, u) \rangle$$

is selected in a node in an iterated MATCH tree, then the selected pairs in part of a descendant branch could be

$$\{\langle \lambda uv.f(f(x, \lambda g.h(u, v(u, d(u)))), \lambda x.e(x)), \ \lambda uv.v(u, u) \rangle\} \overset{\pi_0}{\rightarrow}$$
$$\{\langle \lambda uv.e(h_1(h(u, v(u, d(u))), \lambda x.e(x))), \ \lambda uv.v(u, u) \rangle\} \overset{\pi_1}{\rightarrow}$$
$$\{\langle \lambda uv.h_1(h(u, v(u, d(u))), \lambda x.x), \ \lambda uv.v(u, u) \rangle\} \overset{\pi_2}{\rightarrow}$$
$$\{\langle \lambda uv.h(u, v(u, d(u))), \ \lambda uv.v(u, u) \rangle\} \overset{\pi_3}{\rightarrow}$$
$$\{\langle \lambda uv.v(u, d(u)), \ \lambda uv.v(u, u) \rangle\}$$

at which point, SIMPL can decompose terms. The projection substitutions used in this example are:

$$\pi_0 = \langle f, \ \lambda w_1 w_2.w_2(h_1(w_1, w_2)) \rangle$$
$$\pi_1 = \langle e, \ \lambda w_3.w_3 \rangle$$
$$\pi_2 = \langle h_1, \ \lambda w_4 w_5.w_4 \rangle$$
$$\pi_3 = \langle h, \ \lambda w_6 w_7.w_7 \rangle$$

○

Definition 4.44 A decomposition node or *d-node* of a MATCH tree is either

- The root of the MATCH tree, or

- A node where SIMPL has decomposed the instance of the selected pair of its parent node.

Projections can recur in part of a branch of an iterated MATCH tree between d-nodes. We wish to avoid this form of redundancy and to maintain completeness. We shall define such recurrent projections after this example.

Example 4.45 We write the flexible terms in a sequence of projections between d-nodes in an iterated MATCH tree:

$$\lambda uv.f(\lambda xy.x(y(u))) \longrightarrow$$
$$\lambda uv.h_1(\lambda xy.x(y(u)), h_2(\lambda xy.x(y(u)), u)) \longrightarrow$$
$$\lambda uv.h_2(\lambda xy.x(y(u)), u) \longrightarrow$$
$$\lambda uv.h_3(\lambda xy.x(y(u)), u, h_4(\lambda xy.x(y(u)), u, u)) \longrightarrow$$
$$\lambda uv.h_4(\lambda xy.x(y(u)), u, u)$$

The last projection is a recurrence of the second projection in the sequence. ○

We introduce tags on terms and subterms to identify recurring projections and to analyze the structure of terms formed by applying projection substitutions.

Definition 4.46 A term t is a *tagged* term if for every $i \in \mathcal{O}(t)$ the term t/i has an occurrence associated with it which is called the *tag* of t/i. If r is a tagged term then $tag(r)$ is its tag.

Tagged terms satisfy the following properties:

- $r_1 \triangleright_\alpha r_2$ implies for every $i \in \mathcal{O}(r_1)$, $tag(r_1/i)$ is $tag(r_2/i)$.

- If π is the projection substitution of the form $\{\langle f, s \rangle\}$ for a tagged term r, then in forming $r\pi$ by finding the β-normal form of $(\lambda f.r\ s)$,

  - if x is a variable being replaced by a term t whose head is an introduced variable in s, then $tag(t)$ becomes $tag(x)$.

  - if x is an untagged variable being replaced by a tagged term t, then the tag of t is unchanged.

Example 4.47 If r is the tagged term

$$\lambda uv.f(f(x, \lambda g.h(u, v(u))), \lambda x.x(u))$$

where for every $i \in \mathcal{O}(r)$, $tag(r/i) = i$, and π is the projection substitution

$$\{\langle f, \lambda w_1 w_2.w_2(\lambda y.h_1(w_1, w_2, y)) \rangle\}$$

then $r\pi$ is the term $\lambda uv.h_1(h(u, v(u)), \lambda x.x(u), u)$ where

$$
\begin{aligned}
tag(r\pi) &= tag(r) = \epsilon \\
tag((r\pi)/0.0.0.0.1) &= tag(h(u, v(u))) = 0.0.0.1.1.0 \\
tag((r\pi)/(0.0.0.0.1.0.1)) &= 0.0.0.1.1.0.0.1 \\
tag((r\pi)/(0.0.0.0.1.1)) &= 0.0.0.1.1.0.1 \\
tag((r\pi)/(0.0.0.0.1.1.1)) &= 0.0.0.1.1.0.1.1 \\
tag((r\pi)/(0.0.0.1)) &= tag(\lambda x.x(u)) = tag(r/0.0.1) = 0.0.1 \\
tag((r\pi)/(0.0.0.1.0.1)) &= 0.0.1.0.1 \\
tag((r\pi)/(0.0.1)) &= tag(u) = tag(r/(0.0.1.0.1)) = 0.0.1.0.1
\end{aligned}
$$

$\bigcirc$

We can now define a recurrent projection.

Definition 4.48 If $\langle s, t \rangle$ is a selected pair of a d-node of a MATCH tree where s is the flexible term, then every subterm of s is tagged by its occurrence.

A *label* of an edge in a MATCH tree is a pair of the form (i, j) where i is the tag of the matrix[5] of the flexible term in the pair chosen from the source of the edge, and j is the tag of the matrix of its projectile.

A projection is *recurrent* between d-nodes if and only if the label on the edge corresponding to the projection occurs on an earlier edge after the d-node nearer to the root.

---

[5]See Notation 2.29.

Example 4.49 If $\lambda uv.f(\lambda xy.x(y(u)))$ is the flexible term in the disagreement pair selected in the d-node nearer to the root of the MATCH tree, then using Example 4.45, a sequence of flexible terms in a labelled descendant branch is:

$$\lambda uv.f(\lambda xy.x(y(u))) \longrightarrow_{(0.0,0.0.1.0.0)}$$
$$\lambda uv.h_1(\lambda xy.x(y(u)), h_2(\lambda xy.x(y(u)), u)) \longrightarrow_{(0.0.1.0.0,0.0.1.0.0.1)}$$
$$\lambda uv.h_2(\lambda xy.x(y(u)), u) \longrightarrow_{(0.0.1.0.0.1,0.0.1.0.0)}$$
$$\lambda uv.h_3(\lambda xy.x(y(u)), u, h_4(\lambda xy.x(y(u)), u, u)) \longrightarrow_{(0.0.1.0.0,0.0.1.0.0.1)}$$
$$\lambda uv.h_4(\lambda xy.x(y(u)), u, u)$$

The last projection is a recurrent projection because the label

$$(0.0.1.0.0, 0.0.1.0.0.1)$$

is also the label of the second edge in the sequence. $\bigcirc$

From these definitions, we can make the following general observations about projections.

Proposition 4.50 *If.(i,j) is the label of an edge between consecutive d-nodes of an iterated MATCH tree and s/i is a free variable in the flexible term of the pair selected from the d-node nearer to the root, then there is no other label of the form (i,k) between these d-nodes.*

Proof: Once a projection substitution π has been applied to the flexible term s in the pair selected from the source of the edge labelled (i,j), there can be no subterms with tag i in $s\pi$. $\square$

This implies that the head of a flexible term just before and after a recurrent projection is applied is an introduced variable. It also implies that the projection just before a d-node is reached is never a recurrent projection.

Corollary 4.51 *Between two consecutive d-nodes on a branch of an iterated MATCH tree, if there is a recurrent projection corresponding to an edge labelled (i,j) then the head of s/i is a bound variable in the flexible term s of the disagreement pair selected from the d-node nearer to the root of the MATCH tree.*

Example 4.52 In Example 4.49, the recurrent projection has label $(1,1.1)$. The flexible term $\lambda uv.f(\lambda xy.x(y(u)))$ is in the selected disagreement pair in the d-node nearer to the root. The subterm at occurrence 1 is $\lambda xy.x(y(u))$ whose head x is a bound variable in the flexible term. $\bigcirc$

The following definition is used to avoid recurrent projections.

Definition 4.53 A branch of an iterated MATCH tree is a *truncated branch* if it has been pruned at the edge closest to the root corresponding to a recurrent projection between d-nodes. An iterated MATCH tree is a *truncated MATCH tree* if every branch in the MATCH tree is a truncated branch.

Lemma 4.54 *Every truncated MATCH tree is a finite tree.*

Proof: A truncated MATCH tree can only be infinite if it has an infinite branch which does not contain any recurrent projections. It also must have no d-nodes after a fixed depth because decomposition strictly reduces the total size of rigid terms.

All labels on a branch after the last d-node must be pairs of occurrences in the flexible term of its selected pair. If there are n such occurrences there can be at most n^2 such pairs. This leads to the contradiction that there must be recurrent projections. □

This suggests a sound and terminating matching procedure which truncates a partially generated branch when a recurrent projection is detected. This is done by checking for a repetition of the label of an edge up to the last d-node. Allowing constant symbols in terms does not present a difficulty because the direct descendant of a node where an imitation substitution has been applied is always a d-node.

The Matching Algorithm

The algorithm we describe is for higher-order matching of simply typed terms which can contain constant symbols. We conjecture that this algorithm is complete.

It is a modification of the procedure for higher-order unification discussed in Section 4.2. The algorithm allows non-deterministic selection of a disagreement pair. Iterated MATCH trees become a special case which are useful for analyzing completeness. The procedure can also be applied to higher-order unification problems, but it may not terminate for them.

> *SIMPL is modified by including a tagging phase. A tagging phase is done only at a d-node. It takes a d-node $\{\langle s_1, t_1 \rangle, \dots, \langle s_n, t_n \rangle\}$ where the s_i are flexible terms and returns a tagged d-node by doing the following operations.*
>
> - *For every $j \in \mathcal{O}(s_i)$, tag s_i/j by (j, i) where $1 \leq i \leq n$.*
>
> - *Mark the resulting node N as $N*$ to indicate that it is a d-node.*
>
> *Tags have an extra component in this treatment to identify which pair has been selected from a node.*
>
>   *MATCH includes the projection and imitation rules. Any pair can be selected from a node. To apply the projection rule on a flexible term with tag (j_1, i_1) whose projectile has tag (j_2, i_2), check that the label $((j_1, i_1), (j_2, i_2))$ does not occur on an edge in the branch back to the previous d-node (indicated by the mark '$*$'). If it does not occur, the descendant node is formed and its edge is labelled by $((j_1, i_1), (j_2, i_2))$. Tagging of introduced variables follows Definition 4.46. If it does occur, then a descendant node is not produced using this projection.*

Lemma 4.55 *The higher-order matching procedure is sound and terminating for higher-*
-order matching problems.

Proof: Soundness is immediate from the soundness of the procedure in Section 4.2 and
the observation that its MATCH trees differ because some branches developed by the
original procedure are not truncated. Termination is a direct consequence of Lemma 4.54
and that an application of the imitation rule yields a d-node. □

The use of tags in the modified unification procedure correctly recognizes cycles for the
examples in Section 4.4.1. For all other examples tested, it finds matching substitutions
when they exist. For second-order matching problems, the procedure does not truncate
branches and it reduces to Huet and Lang's algorithm [103] with tagging.

To show that higher-order matching is decidable, it remains to show that this algorithm
will not find a matching substitution if and only if the initial higher-order matching
problem is insoluble. This result would also show that the procedure can heuristically
prune branches of MATCH trees for higher-order unification problems.

We have shown that decidability can be determined by merely considering part of a
branch between d-nodes of an iterated MATCH tree for a pure matching problem. This
reduction and the introduction of tagging perhaps makes it more likely that further results
can be found by this approach.

We now give four other approaches for resolving the question of the decidability of
higher-order matching: the Plotkin-Statman Conjecture; two decidable third-order problems and their complexities; and a discussion of how Zaionc's analogy of unification with
regular grammars may be applicable.

Classes of decidable higher-order matching problems do not seem to have been defined
before. The two decidable third-order problems we present seem to be the first to be
discussed.

4.4.4 Plotkin-Statman Conjecture

R. Statman [185] reduced the decidability of higher-order matching of pure simply typed λ-
-terms to the decidability of λ-definability. We relate the definitions to those in Section 3.3
on model theory for higher-order logic.

Definition 4.56 When $T_0 = \{\iota\}$, the frame of a standard model is a *full type hierarchy*.

Closed pure terms always have a denotation in a full type hierarchy. Only such terms
are considered.

G.D. Plotkin [157] has conjectured it is decidable whether a function is λ-definable
(Definition 3.19) in the full type hierarchy when $\mathcal{D}_\iota$ is finite. This is called 'Plotkin's λ-
-Definability Conjecture' by Statman [185], and 'Statman's Conjecture' by Plotkin [159].
Statman [186] has described verifying the Conjecture as "The outstanding open problem
in the model theory of the typed λ-calculus".

Plotkin [158] proved the following completeness theorem which semantically charac-
terizes λ-definability. If this theorem holds when $\mathcal{D}_\iota$ is finite, then it implies the Plotkin-
-Statman Conjecture [159].

Theorem 4.57 *(Plotkin.) Suppose $\mathcal{D}_\iota$ is infinite. Then an element d of $\mathcal{D}_\alpha$ is λ-definable if and only if it I-satisfies every I-relation $R \subseteq \mathcal{D}_\iota^3 \times W$.*

In the theorem, the relation R is interpreted intuitionistically in the sense of Kripke [118]. The set W is a set of worlds which is ordered by a reflexive and transitive relation $\leq$. The I-relation R has the property:

$$R(d, d, d, w) \supset \forall w' : ((w \leq w') \supset R(d, d, d, w'))$$

for all $d \in \mathcal{D}_\iota$. An element $d \in \mathcal{D}_\iota$ I-satisfies such an I-relation if $R(d, d, d, w)$ holds for all $w \in W$.

Most of the proof of the theorem involves constructing a suitable I-relation R, and set of worlds W. It relies on another theorem (Theorem 3) which does not hold if $\mathcal{D}_\iota$ is finite. It seems that a proof of such a completeness theorem assuming that $\mathcal{D}_\iota$ is finite will not be found by directly modifying Plotkin's proof.

Relating the decidability of higher-order matching to the Plotkin-Statman Conjecture depends on the *Finite Completeness Theorem*, proved by Statman [185].

Theorem 4.58 *For each closed term t there is a positive integer m effectively computable from t such that $s =_{\beta\eta} t$ for any term s if and only if the denotations of t and s are equal in the full type hierarchy where $|\mathcal{D}_\iota| = m$.*

Statman states the higher-order matching problem in this form: given closed terms t and u where $\tau(t) = (\alpha_1, \ldots, \alpha_n \to \beta)$ and $\tau(u) = \beta$, do there exist closed terms $s_1, \ldots, s_n$ where $\tau(s_i) = \alpha_i$ for $1 \leq i \leq n$ such that $t(s_1, \ldots, s_n) =_{\beta\eta} u$? This is called the *range question*. He notes that there is no loss of generality by considering t and u to be closed terms or by not considering sets of pairs of such terms.

Theorem 4.59 *(Statman.) The Plotkin-Statman Conjecture implies the range question is decidable.*

Proof: From Theorem 4.58, we can effectively compute m from u. The domains are finite sets in the full type hierarchy when $\mathcal{D}_\iota$ is finite. Using the full type hierarchy when $|\mathcal{D}_\iota| = m$, we can search through every tuple from the finite set $\mathcal{D}_{\alpha_1} \times \cdots \times \mathcal{D}_{\alpha_n}$.

If ever a tuple $(x_1, \ldots, x_n)$ is found such that the denotation of t applied to $(x_1, \ldots, x_n)$ is the denotation of u, then assuming the Plotkin-Statman Conjecture we can decide if there are n closed terms whose denotations are the x_i. If ever such terms exist, then by Theorem 4.58 the range question is answered affirmatively. $\square$

The decidability of the range question is one of several model theoretic and computational complexity consequences of the Plotkin-Statman Conjecture presented by Statman [185]. If the range question were not decidable, the Plotkin-Statman Conjecture would be false and the derivations of its other consequences would be invalid.

Statman [187] has told me that the Conjecture is equivalent to the pattern matching problem with delta functions.

We introduce definitions for a specialized simply typed λ-calculus.

Definition 4.60 Let $c_1, \ldots, c_n$ be distinct constant symbols of type ι and Δ a constant symbol of type $(\iota, \iota, \iota, \iota \to \iota)$. Let t be a term of the simply typed λ-calculus where $\{\Delta, c_1, \ldots, c_n\} \subseteq C$ and t/i has the form $\Delta(c_i, c_j, c_k, c_l)$ where $i \in \mathcal{O}(t)$.

The term $t[i \leftarrow c']$ follows from t by the rule of δ-*Reduction* where c' is c_k if $i = j$, and c' is c_l if $i \neq j$, and $1 \leq i, j, k, l \leq n$.

We now define the $\lambda\delta$-calculus.

Definition 4.61 The $\lambda\delta$-calculus consists of simply typed terms over

$$C = \{\Delta, c_1, \ldots, c_n\}$$

where $\tau(c_i) = \iota$ and $n \geq 1$, and the rules of α-conversion, β-, η-, and δ-reduction.

The pattern matching problem with delta functions is the following problem.

Definition 4.62 Let s and t be two closed terms of the $\lambda\delta$-calculus where $\tau(s) = (\alpha \to \iota)$ and $\tau(t) = \iota$. The *pattern matching problem with delta functions* is the problem of deciding whether there is a closed term r of the pure λ-calculus such that $(s \ r)$ is t.

The relation of this problem to the Plotkin-Statman Conjecture is given by the following theorem.

Theorem 4.63 (*Statman.*) *The pattern matching problem with delta functions is decidable if and only if the Plotkin-Statman Conjecture is true.*

Proof: The first part of the proof of this result depends on the Finite Completeness Theorem for the $\lambda\delta$-calculus which is analogous to the Finite Completeness Theorem (Theorem 4.58), and it is proved in a similar way. Also, similarly to the proof of Theorem 4.59, it follows that the Conjecture implies the pattern matching problem with delta functions is decidable.

To decide whether a function $g \in \mathcal{D}_\alpha$ is the denotation of a pure closed λ-term without delta functions, choose any functions $f \in \mathcal{D}_{(\alpha \to \iota)}$ and $h \in \mathcal{D}_\iota$ such that $(f \ g)$ is h. Church observed that every function in the full type hierarchy is the denotation of some effectively computable term of the $\lambda\delta$-calculus. Thus we can find terms s and t in the $\lambda\delta$-calculus whose denotations in the hierarchy are f and h, respectively. It follows that g is the denotation of a closed term r of the pure λ-calculus if and only if there is a solution to finding whether there is a term r such that $(s \ r)$ is t. If the pattern matching problem with delta functions is decidable, then the Plotkin-Statman Conjecture is true. $\square$

One way to resolve the decidability of higher-order matching is to try to reduce Hilbert's Tenth Problem to it. If we use pure simply typed Church numerals then variables, multiplication, and addition are all λ-definable as in the reduction for third-order equational matching in Section 4.1.3.

The reduction for higher-order matching is only possible if equality of simply typed Church numerals or subtraction of them are λ-definable. However, equality of simply typed Church numerals or any other pure simply typed numerals of a fixed type is not λ-definable [60].

This is a consequence of the fact that all domains are finite in a full type hierarchy when $\mathcal{D}_\iota$ is a finite set. In such a full type hierarchy, there must exist representations of distinct numerals whose denotations are the same[6]. This makes it unlikely that there is a reduction from Hilbert's Tenth Problem.

4.4.5   Decidable Matching Problems

Decidable Third-Order Problems

Pure higher-order matching is another special case of higher-order equational unification[7]. Schwichtenberg [171] (and R. Statman [183], independently) have shown that the λ--definable functions on the simply typed Church numerals in pure simply typed λ-calculus are exactly the extended polynomials.

Definition 4.64 The functions sg and $\overline{sg}$ are the following functions on the non-negative integers:

$$sg(x) = \begin{cases} 0 & \text{if } x = 0 \\ 1 & \text{if } x > 0. \end{cases}$$

$$\overline{sg}(x) = \begin{cases} 0 & \text{if } x > 0 \\ 1 & \text{if } x = 0. \end{cases}$$

An *extended polynomial* is a polynomial built up from 0, 1, +, ×, sg, and $\overline{sg}$.

These functions are λ-definable in pure simply typed λ-calculus. To λ-define sg and $\overline{sg}$ we shall use a dyad combinator [40].

Definition 4.65 A *dyad combinator* is a term of type $(N, N, N \rightarrow N)$ with the property

$$DXY\overline{0} = X$$

$$DXY\overline{(n+1)} = Y$$

where X and Y are simply typed Church numerals.

Proposition 4.66 *In pure simply typed λ-calculus the dyad combinator can be defined by*

$$D = \lambda uvxyz.x(\lambda t.v(y, z), u(y, z))$$

with type $(N, N, N \rightarrow N)$.

---

[6]This was told to me by J.C. Mitchell [141] who states that he heard it from Plotkin who said he got the idea from Statman. The observation that equality is not λ-definable in pure simply typed λ-calculus is also attributed to Statman by Fortune et al. [60].

[7]It has recently been shown that third-order matching is decidable in general [48], which is in agreement with the results of this Section.

Proof: Testing the cases of Definition 4.65 gives:

$$\lambda uvxyz.x(\lambda t.v(y,z), u(y,z))XY(\lambda x_1y_1.y_1) \;\triangleright_\beta\; \lambda yz.X(y,z) \;\triangleright_\eta\; X$$

and

$$\lambda uvxyz.x(\lambda t.v(y,z), u(y,z))XY(\lambda x_1y_1.\;\underbrace{x_1(\cdots x_1}_{n+1}(y_1)\cdots)) \;\triangleright_\beta$$

$$\lambda yz.(\underbrace{\lambda t.Y(y,z)(\cdots \lambda t.Y(y,z)}_{n+1}(X(y,z))\cdots))$$

$$\triangleright_\beta \lambda yz.Y(y,z) \;\triangleright_\eta\; Y$$

□

We can now define the representations of sg and $\overline{sg}$. We recall that the λ-definitions of a non-negative integer constant, a numerical variable, $\times$, and $+$ were given in Definition 4.24.

Definition 4.67 The representation of

- sg is $\lambda x.\mathrm{D}(\overline{0},\overline{1},x)$ with type $(N \to N)$.

- $\overline{sg}$ is $\lambda x.\mathrm{D}(\overline{1},\overline{0},x)$ with type $(N \to N)$.

Proposition 4.68 *Every extended polynomial can be effectively encoded as a pure simply typed λ-term of type N.*

Proof: This is immediate by structural induction on the extended polynomial and by applications of the representations in Definitions 4.24 and 4.67. □

The class of non-trivial decidable higher-order matching problems we shall define is based on an encoding of the problem in the next theorem.

Proposition 4.69 *The problem*

$$\exists x_1 \cdots x_n \, (p(x_1,\ldots,x_n) = c)$$

is decidable, where p is an extended polynomial over the variables x_i, and c is a non-negative integer constant.

Proof: If $\exists x_1 \cdots x_n p(x_1,\ldots,x_n) = c$ holds then by structural induction it holds when the x_i are in the range $0 \le x_i \le c$ where $1 \le i \le n$. Therefore, the problem is decidable because it is necessary to test at most $(c+1)^n$ evaluations. □

To encode $\exists x_1 \cdots x_n p(x_1,\ldots,x_n) = c$ as a higher-order matching problem, form the disagreement set $\{\langle \overline{p(x_1,\ldots,x_n)}, \overline{c}\rangle\}$, where $\overline{p(x_1,\ldots,x_n)}$ is the encoding of $p(x_1,\ldots,x_n)$ using the observation of Proposition 4.68.

This gives a non-trivial class of decidable higher-order matching problems.

Theorem 4.70 *The higher-order matching problem*

$$\{\langle \overline{p(x_1, \ldots, x_n)}, \overline{c}\rangle\}$$

has a solution if and only if $\exists x_1 \cdots x_n p(x_1, \ldots, x_n) = c$ *has a solution.*

Proof: If θ is a solution to the matching problem then $x_i\theta$ must be a simply typed Church numeral $\overline{c_i}$ where $1 \leq i \leq n$ because in β-normal form all pure closed simply typed terms of type N are Church numerals [183]. It follows that $p(c_1, \ldots, c_n) = c$. The converse is immediate. $\square$

Pure Matchability is NP-Hard

We now show that pure third-order matchability is NP-hard by a polynomial reduction from the problem of propositional satisfiability. Complexity results for pure higher-order matchability do not seem to have been discussed before[8].

The main technique is to encode propositional formulas by using the dyad combinator D of Proposition 4.66 and the encodings in Definition 4.24.

Definition 4.71 The following encodings are used:

- Propositional variable: $enc\, x = \mathsf{D}\overline{0}\,\overline{1}\overline{x}$, where $\overline{x} = \lambda uv.x(\lambda t.u(t), v)$ with type N.

- Conjunction: $enc\,(x \wedge y) = \mathsf{D}\overline{0}\,\overline{1}(enc\, x \;\overline{\times}\; enc\, y)$.

- Disjunction: $enc\,(x \vee y) = \mathsf{D}\overline{0}\,\overline{1}(enc\, x \;\overline{\mp}\; enc\, y)$.

- Negation: $enc\,(\neg x) = \mathsf{D}\overline{1}\,\overline{0}\,(enc\, x)$.

We show that for any propositional formula X, with representation $enc\, X$ as a pure third-order simply typed λ-term, the pure third-order matchability problem $\{\langle enc\, X, \overline{1}\rangle\}$ has a solution if and only if X is satisfiable.

This leads to the following theorem.

Theorem 4.72 *Pure third-order matchability is NP-hard.*

Proof: Let $enc\, X$ be the representation as a pure simply typed λ-term of a propositional formula X. It is immediate by structural induction on X that $enc\, X$ can be constructed in polynomial time.

By the Schwichtenberg-Statman result [171, 183], $enc\, X$ is an extended polynomial. By Theorem 4.70, $\{\langle enc\, X, \overline{1}\rangle\}$ has a solution if and only if X is satisfiable. $\square$

---

[8]Paliath Narendran has told me that L.D. Baxter has shown that second-order matchability with constant symbols is NP-hard by a reduction from the problem of **ONE-IN-THREE SATISFIABIL-ITY** [170].

The Projection Property

The projection property is based on the effect of projection substitutions. These substitutions were defined in Definition 4.34.

Definition 4.73 Given a term $t = \lambda x_1 \cdots x_n.@(t_1, \ldots, t_m)$, the *projection property* holds if and only if there exists a substitution π such that $head(t\pi) = x_i$ where $1 \leq i \leq n$.

If this property does not hold for a disagreement pair in a matching problem where the head of the rigid term corresponds to x_i, then the matching problem has no solution. More strongly, if the projection property is undecidable then higher-order matching is undecidable. We conjecture that the projection property is decidable if and only if higher--order matching is decidable.

Sometimes it is possible to predict when the projection property holds, and this depends on the form of a sequence of subterms.

Definition 4.74 A sequence

$$\lambda x_1 \cdots x_n.@(t_1, \ldots, t_m) = E_1, E_2, \ldots, E_k$$

of terms is a *projection path* for x_i where $1 \leq i \leq n$ if and only if:

- E_j is an immediate subterm of E_{j-1} where $2 \leq j \leq k$.

- $head(E_k) = x_i$.

- There is no $l : 1 \leq l < k$ such that $head(E_l) \in \{x_1, \ldots x_n\}$.

Example 4.75 A projection path for v is:

$$\lambda uv.f(f(x, \lambda g.h(v, u)), \lambda x.h(x, v)),$$
$$f(x, \lambda g.h(v, u)),$$
$$\lambda g.h(v, u),$$
$$v$$

There are two kinds of projection path, and they are defined below.

Definition 4.76 A projection path $E_1, \ldots, E_k$ is *unmixed* if and only if whenever $head(E_i) = head(E_j)$ where $1 \leq i < j \leq k$, E_{i+1} and E_{j+1} are corresponding immediate subterms. A projection path is a *mixed* projection path if and only if it is not an unmixed projection path.

We can make correct predictions about the projection property for the former kind of projection path.

Lemma 4.77 The projection property holds for x in a term t if there is an unmixed projection path for x in t.

Example 4.78 The term $\lambda uv.f(\lambda x.f(\lambda g.h(v,u),x),y)$ has an unmixed projection path for v. The projection property holds for v with the substitution

$$\pi = \{\langle f,\ \lambda w_1 w_2.w_1(h_1(w_1,w_2)) \rangle,\ \langle h,\ \lambda w_3 w_4.w_3 \rangle\}.$$

○

Remark 4.79 The projection property can hold for mixed projection paths. It holds for v in $\lambda uv.f(f(x,\lambda g.h(v,u)),\lambda x.h(x,v))$ with the substitution

$$\pi = \{\langle f,\ \lambda w_1 w_2.w_2(w_1) \rangle,\ \langle h,\ \lambda w_3 w_4.w_3 \rangle\}.$$

We now define a form of matching problem for which the projection property holds.

Lemma 4.80 *The projection property holds provided that for all variables f where $\tau(f) = (\alpha_1,\ldots,\alpha_n \rightarrow \beta)$ and β is a base type we have $\alpha_i = \alpha_j$ if and only if $i = j$ where $1 \leq i,j \leq n$.*

Proof: The condition on types in Lemma 4.80 ensures that all projection paths are unmixed. □

4.4.6   Regular Unification Problems

M. Zaionc [203] presented a characterization of a set of unifiers of a pair of terms of restricted types by regular expressions. He gave a procedure for *approximating* a set of unifiers by constructing regular expressions from a tree related to the MATCH tree of Huet's [97] procedure discussed in Section 4.2.

The construction does not imply that the unifiability of such terms is decidable, and it is not clear which set of unifiers is being approximated; there are comments in the paper about 'most general unifiers', but these no longer exist [98], and the tree generated by a regular grammar is referred to as a MATCH tree when it is not. However, by considering such restricted cases, insights about the general problem may be found.

Below we give a clarified version of Zaionc's definition of term grammar, their relation to substitutions, and the restriction to regular term grammars. The key observation follows by analogy from a more general result presented by B. Courcelle [38] which is also discussed: the set of unifiers for a regular unification problem can be exactly described by a regular expression associated with its term grammar if and only if the 'parse' tree for the regular unification problem is a regular tree. For cases where exact regular expressions exist, Zaionc's procedure may give an effective means to compute them.

For every set Y of variables and type α, let

$$Cl(\alpha,Y) = \{t\,|\,(\tau(t) = \alpha) \wedge (\mathcal{F}(t) \subseteq Y)\}$$

and $Cl(\alpha) = Cl(\alpha,\emptyset)$.

Definition 4.81 A *term grammar* is denoted $G = (V, T, P, S)$ where V is a finite set of *nonterminals* each of which is a variable, and T is a set of *terminals* each of which is a closed term. The set P is a finite set of *productions* each of which has the form $y \rightarrow t$ where $y \in V$, $\tau(y) = \tau(t) = \alpha$, and $t \in Cl(\alpha, V)$. The symbol S is a special nonterminal which is called the *start symbol*. A term grammar G is *regular* if the right side of every production in P has at most one occurrence of a nonterminal.

Definition 4.82 Let $y \rightarrow t$ be a production in a term grammar G, and suppose that s is any term such that $i \in \mathcal{O}(s)$ and s/i is y, then s *directly derives* $s[i \leftarrow t]$ in grammar G, or

$$s \Rightarrow_G s[i \leftarrow t].$$

The relation $\stackrel{*}{\Rightarrow}_G$ is defined as the reflexive and transitive closure of the relation $\Rightarrow_G$.

The *language generated* by G is $\{N \mid S \stackrel{*}{\Rightarrow}_G N \wedge N \in T\}$.

Let $G = (V, T, P, S)$ be a term grammar. Each production in P can be given a unique *label*. The collection of such labels forms an *alphabet* Σ_G.

Every *word* in Σ_G^* can be mapped to a substitution using the function $\mathcal{I}$ which we now define.

Definition 4.83 The function $\mathcal{I}$ is defined by:

1. $\mathcal{I}(\epsilon) = \emptyset$, where ϵ is the empty word.

2. $\mathcal{I}(a \cdot w) = \{\langle x, t \rangle\} \circ \mathcal{I}(w)$, where a is the label of production $x \rightarrow t$ from P, $\cdot$ is the function which concatenates words, $w \in \Sigma_G^*$, and $\circ$ is substitution composition.

The function $\mathcal{I}$ is well-defined because composition of substitutions is an associative operation [97].

Regular Types

To define regular types, we first introduce some convenient definitions about types.

Definition 4.84 *The* arity of a type $|\alpha|$ *of* $[\alpha = (\alpha_1, \ldots, \alpha_n \rightarrow \beta)$ *where* $\beta \in T_0$ *is* n.

The next two definitions generalize those in Huet [100].

Definition 4.85 *The* type occurrences of a type α, $\mathcal{O}\tau(\alpha)$ *is the smallest set of occurrences formed using the rules:*

1. $\epsilon \in \mathcal{O}\tau(\alpha)$.

2. $i.j \in \mathcal{O}\tau(\alpha)$ *if* α *is of the form* $(\alpha_1, \ldots, \alpha_n \rightarrow \beta)$ *where* $\beta \in T_0$, $1 \leq i \leq n$, *and* $j \in \mathcal{O}\tau(\alpha_i)$.

Definition 4.86 *The* subtype of α at type occurrence i, *where* $i \in \mathcal{O}\tau(\alpha)$ *is written* α/i *and it is*

1. α *if* $i = \epsilon$.

2. α_j/k *if* α *is of the form* $(\alpha_1, \ldots, \alpha_n \to \beta)$ *where* $1 \le i \le n$, $\beta \in T_0$ *and* $i = j.k$ *where* $1 \le j \le n$.

M. Zaionc [203] defines a type α to be a regular type if and only if

$$order_{unif}(\alpha) \le 4 \text{ and } \forall i : (1 \le i \le |\alpha|) \ |\alpha/i| \le 1.$$

This implies that α/i where $1 \le i \le |\alpha|$ is one of the following types:

- o.

- $(o \to o)$.

- $(((\underbrace{o, \ldots, o}_{n}) \to o) \to o)$ where $n \ge 1$.

Zaionc [203] proves the following theorem:

Theorem 4.87 *For every regular type, there exists a regular grammar generating all closed terms having that type.*

We note that this result applies only to the pure typed λ-calculus. The proof constructs a regular grammar. When α is a regular type and $\exists i : (1 \le i \le |\alpha|)$ such that $\alpha/i = o$ the productions of the regular grammar are as follows.

a_i. $y \Rightarrow \lambda x_1 \cdots x_n.x_i$ for every i such that $1 \le i \le |\alpha|$ and $\alpha/i = o$.

b_i. $y \Rightarrow \lambda x_1 \cdots x_n.x_i(y(x_1, \ldots, x_n))$ for every i such that $1 \le i \le |\alpha|$ and $\alpha/i = (o \to o)$.

c_i. $y \Rightarrow \lambda x_1 \cdots x_n.x_i(\lambda z_1 \cdots z_p.y(x_1, \ldots, x_n))$ for every i such that $1 \le i \le |\alpha|$ and $order_{unif}(\alpha/i) = 3$ where $p = |\alpha/(i.1)|$.

c_i^{-r}. $y \Rightarrow \lambda x_1 \cdots x_n.x_i(\lambda z_1 \cdots z_p.y(x_1, \ldots, x_{j-1}, z_r, x_{j+1}, \ldots, x_n))$ for every i such that $1 \le i \le |\alpha|$ and every r such that $r \le |\alpha/(i.1)| = p$, $order_{unif}(\alpha/i) = 3$, and j is the greatest occurrence such that $\alpha/j = o$ and $1 \le j \le |\alpha|$.

The start symbol is y. This regular grammar has $n + \Sigma_{i \in occ_3}|\alpha/(i.1)|$ productions where $occ_3 = \{i \mid (1 \le i \le |\alpha|) \wedge order_{unif}(\alpha/i) = 3\}$.

When α is a regular type such that $\neg \exists i : (1 \le i \le |\alpha|)\alpha/i = o$, the set of nonterminals is $\{y_1, y_2\}$ where $\tau(y_1) = \alpha$ and $\tau(y_2) = (\alpha/1, \ldots, \alpha/|\alpha|, o \to o)$. The productions of the associated regular grammar consist of the previous productions for y_2 and the following productions for y_1:

d_i. $y_1 \Rightarrow \lambda x_1 \cdots x_n.x_i(y_1(x_1, \ldots, x_n))$ for every i such that $1 \le i \le |\alpha|$ and $\alpha/i = (o \to o)$.

e_i. $y_1 \Rightarrow \lambda x_1 \cdots x_n.x_i(\lambda z_1 \cdots z_p.y_2(x_1, \ldots, x_n, z_r)$ for every i such that $1 \le i \le |\alpha|$ and every r such that $order_{unif}(\alpha/i) = 3$ and $r \le |\alpha/(i.1)| = p$.

The start symbol is y_1. The number of productions is

$$2(n + \Sigma_{i \in occ_3} |\alpha/(i.1)|) + 1 - |\ occ_3\ |.$$

For example, the productions of the regular grammar for the type

$$((o \to o), ((o, o \to o) \to o), ((o, o, o \to o) \to o), (o \to o) \to o)$$

are:

$$
\begin{array}{lll}
y_2 & \Rightarrow & \lambda u_1 v_1 v_2 u_2 w_1 . w_1 & a_5 \\
y_2 & \Rightarrow & \lambda u_1 v_1 v_2 u_2 w_1 . u_1 (y_2(u_1, v_1, v_2, u_2, w_1)) & b_1 \\
y_2 & \Rightarrow & \lambda u_1 v_1 v_2 u_2 w_1 . u_2 (y_2(u_1, v_1, v_2, u_2, w_1)) & b_4 \\
y_2 & \Rightarrow & \lambda u_1 v_1 v_2 u_2 w_1 . v_1 (\lambda z_1 z_2 . y_2(u_1, v_1, v_2, u_2, w_1)) & c_2 \\
y_2 & \Rightarrow & \lambda u_1 v_1 v_2 u_2 w_1 . v_2 (\lambda z_1 z_2 z_3 . y_2(u_1, v_1, v_2, u_2, w_1)) & c_3 \\
y_2 & \Rightarrow & \lambda u_1 v_1 v_2 u_2 w_1 . v_1 (\lambda z_1 z_2 . y_2(u_1, v_1, v_2, u_2, z_1)) & c_2^{-1} \\
y_2 & \Rightarrow & \lambda u_1 v_1 v_2 u_2 w_1 . v_1 (\lambda z_1 z_2 . y_2(u_1, v_1, v_2, u_2, z_2)) & c_2^{-2} \\
y_2 & \Rightarrow & \lambda u_1 v_1 v_2 u_2 w_1 . v_2 (\lambda z_1 z_2 z_3 . y_2(u_1, v_1, v_2, u_2, z_1)) & c_3^{-1} \\
y_2 & \Rightarrow & \lambda u_1 v_1 v_2 u_2 w_1 . v_2 (\lambda z_1 z_2 z_3 . y_2(u_1, v_1, v_2, u_2, z_2)) & c_3^{-2} \\
y_2 & \Rightarrow & \lambda u_1 v_1 v_2 u_2 w_1 . v_2 (\lambda z_1 z_2 z_3 . y_2(u_1, v_1, v_2, u_2, z_3)) & c_3^{-3} \\
y_1 & \Rightarrow & \lambda u_1 v_1 v_2 u_2 . u_1 (y_1(u_1, v_1, v_2, u_2)) & d_1 \\
y_1 & \Rightarrow & \lambda u_1 v_1 v_2 u_2 . u_2 (y_1(u_1, v_1, v_2, u_2)) & d_4 \\
y_1 & \Rightarrow & \lambda u_1 v_1 v_2 u_2 . v_1 (\lambda z_1 z_2 . y_2(u_1, v_1, v_2, u_2, z_1)) & e_2^{-1} \\
y_1 & \Rightarrow & \lambda u_1 v_1 v_2 u_2 . v_1 (\lambda z_1 z_2 . y_2(u_1, v_1, v_2, u_2, z_2)) & e_2^{-2} \\
y_1 & \Rightarrow & \lambda u_1 v_1 v_2 u_2 . v_2 (\lambda z_1 z_2 z_3 . y_2(u_1, v_1, v_2, u_2, z_1)) & e_3^{-1} \\
y_1 & \Rightarrow & \lambda u_1 v_1 v_2 u_2 . v_2 (\lambda z_1 z_2 z_3 . y_2(u_1, v_1, v_2, u_2, z_2)) & e_3^{-2} \\
y_1 & \Rightarrow & \lambda u_1 v_1 v_2 u_2 . v_2 (\lambda z_1 z_2 z_3 . y_2(u_1, v_1, v_2, u_2, z_3)) & e_3^{-3} \\
\end{array}
$$

The sequence of derivations to produce the closed term

$$\lambda u_1 v_1 v_2 u_2 . u_1 (u_2(v_1(\lambda w_7 w_8 . v_2(\lambda w_9 w_{10} w_{11} . u_2(w_{10})))))$$

is

$$
\begin{aligned}
& y_1 \\
& \lambda u_1 v_1 v_2 u_2 . u_1 (y_1(u_1, v_1, v_2, u_2)) \\
& \lambda u_1 v_1 v_2 u_2 . u_1 (u_2(y_1(u_1, v_1, v_2, u_2))) \\
& \lambda u_1 v_1 v_2 u_2 . u_1 (u_2(v_1(\lambda w_7 w_8 . y_2(u_1, v_1, v_2, u_2, w_7)))) \\
& \lambda u_1 v_1 v_2 u_2 . u_1 (u_2(v_1(\lambda w_7 w_8 . v_2(\lambda w_9 w_{10} w_{11} . y_2(u_1, v_1, v_2, u_2, w_{10}))))) \\
& \lambda u_1 v_1 v_2 u_2 . u_1 (u_2(v_1(\lambda w_7 w_8 . v_2(\lambda w_9 w_{10} w_{11} . u_2(y_2(u_1, v_1, v_2, u_2, w_{10})))))) \\
& \lambda u_1 v_1 v_2 u_2 . u_1 (u_2(v_1(\lambda w_7 w_8 . v_2(\lambda w_9 w_{10} w_{11} . u_2(w_{10}))))) \\
\end{aligned}
$$

using productions $d_1, d_4, e_2^{-1}, c_3^{-2}, b_4$, and a_5, respectively.

Theorem 4.87 leads to the following similar result.

Theorem 4.88 *There exists a regular grammar whose language consists of every closed term formed only from constant symbols $C_1, \ldots, C_n$ where $order_{unif}(C_i) \leq 3$ and $|\tau(C_i)| \leq 1$ for $1 \leq i \leq n$.*

A *regular unification problem* $\{\langle s,t \rangle\}$ is a pair of terms of the same type such that all occurrences of variables in s and t are of regular types, and any occurrence of a constant c satisfies the condition in Theorem 4.88. A regular grammar can be constructed for the regular unification problem, generating all closed terms formed just from the set of constants occurring in s and t using the algorithm in the proof of Theorem 4.88.

A 'parse' tree for the regular unification problem can be formed whose root is $\{\langle s,t \rangle\}$ and whose children are all disagreement sets formed by all direct derivations from the root using the productions in the generated grammar. Zaionc's procedure constructs approximate regular expressions to describe the sequence of labels of productions used from the root of the tree to form each branch. Such a tree is a *regular tree* [38] if the set of all subtrees of the tree is finite.

It follows that if the parse tree for a regular unification problem is regular then the set of all strings of labels of productions used from the root of the tree to a success node is a regular set [38], and it can be described exactly by a regular expression.

To resolve the decidability of regular unification and regular matching it would suffice to show that parse trees are regular, and a parse tree has a success branch if and only if there is a unifier for the problem. Zaionc [204] considers more general term grammars having denumerable sets of productions which can generate all closed pure terms of any type. It can be seen that the algorithm in the proof of Theorem 4.88 also applies for these term grammars, and similar parse trees can be defined.

These techniques for analyzing the decidability of regular matching may give insights about the general case.

4.4.7 Discussion

The Plotkin-Statman Conjecture, the difficulty of reducing Hilbert's Tenth Problem to higher-order matching because equality is not λ-definable, and the decidability of third--order matching and matching problems with unmixed projection paths are consistent with the possibility that the problem is decidable in general, as first suggested by Huet.

Showing the completeness of the higher-order matching algorithm using the tagged terms of Section 4.4.3, and analysing mixed projection paths are approaches which seem most likely to lead to further insights about the problem. A completeness proof would provide a constructive solution which can also be heuristically applied to higher-order unification problems.

4.5 Second-Order Monadic Unification

Apart from restrictions on the order of unification and matching problems, monadic unification and matching additionally places a restriction on the types of variables and constant symbols.

Definition 4.89 A *second-order monadic term* is a second-order term formed only from atoms @ such that $|\tau(@)| \le 1$.

These type restrictions allow us to omit parentheses in second-order monadic terms. Such terms of ground type are strings of variables and constant symbols. We shall also write $@^n$ to abbreviate the n-fold application of the atom $@$ in a term. The analogy with strings leads to the following complexity measure.

Definition 4.90 Let t be a second-order monadic term and $\tau(t) \in T_0$.

$$length(t) = \begin{cases} 1 & \text{if } t \in \mathcal{X} \cup \mathcal{C} \\ 1 + length(t/1) & \text{if } 1 \in \mathcal{O}(t) \end{cases}$$

We now define second-order monadic unification and matching.

Definition 4.91 A unification problem (matching problem) for a disagreement set is a *second-order monadic unification problem (matching problem)* if and only if every term in the disagreement set is a second-order monadic term.

In analyzing the complexity of second-order unification, Huet gave the counterexample in the proof of the following result.

Theorem 4.92 *Let $\{\langle t_1, t_2 \rangle\}$ be a unifiable second-order monadic unification problem. An upper bound on the number of applications of the imitation rule is not given by* $\max\{length(t_1), length(t_2)\}$.

Proof: Let t_1 be $fABABgfABD$ and t_2 be $ABfgABg^nD$. It is easy to verify that the unifier which results in the smallest common instance is

$$\{\langle f, \lambda u.(AB)^{n-1}u \rangle, \langle g, \lambda u.ABu \rangle\}$$

and that the imitation rule must be applied at least $2(n-1)$ times. We have

$$\max\{length(t_1), length(t_2)\} = n + 7$$

for $n \geq 4$. The result follows because $2(n-1) > n + 7$ when $n \geq 10$. $\square$

Winterstein [195] generalized this result as follows.

Theorem 4.93 *Let $\{\langle t_1, t_2 \rangle\}$ be a unifiable second-order monadic unification problem. There does not exist a polynomial upper bound for the number of applications of the imitation rule.*

Proof: The proof shows that m^k is not an upper bound for the number of applications of the imitation rule where k is a fixed natural number and $m = \max\{length(t_1), length(t_2)\}$.

The counterexample uses the pair $\{\langle t_1^k, t_2^k \rangle\}$ where

$$t_1^k = f_k ABf_{k-1}AB \cdots f_1 ABf_0 ABABgf ABD_1 f_0^n D_2 f_1^n \cdots D_k f_{k-1}^n D_{k+1}$$

and

$$t_2^k = ABf_k ABf_{k-1} \cdots ABf_1 ABf_0 gABg^n D_1 f_1 D_2 f_2 \cdots D_k f_k D_{k+1}$$

when $k \geq 0$ and where $f_0, \ldots, f_k$ are distinct variables and $n \geq 2$. When $k = 0$ and $n = 0$ this gives an instance of the pair in Theorem 4.93.

We have $length(t_1) = 4k+nk+10$, and $length(t_2) = 5k+n+7$, so that $m = 4k+nk+10$. It can be verified by induction that a unifier for $\{\langle t_1, t_2 \rangle\}$ resulting after applying the fewest applications of the imitation rule is

$$\{\langle f_0, \lambda u.(AB)^{(n-1)} \rangle, \ldots, \langle f_k, \lambda u.(AB)^{n^k(n-1)} \rangle, \langle g, \lambda u.ABu \rangle\}.$$

It requires $2n^k(n-1)$ applications of the imitation rule to find the substitution for f_k. A natural number n_0 can always be chosen which satisfies $2(n_0-1) > (k+1)^k$ and $n_0 \geq 4k+10$. It follows that $2n_0^k(n_0-1) > (kn_0+4k+10)^k = m^k$, as required. $\square$

4.5.1　Decidability and the Monoid Problem

To discuss the decidability of second-order monadic unification, we need some preliminary definitions before defining a closely related problem, called the monoid problem.

Definition 4.94 $F[C \cup U]$ is the monoid over the union of the set C of coefficients and U of unknowns. Multiplication is $\cdot$ and ϵ is the identity element. An element $a_1 \cdot a_2 \cdots a_n$ of $F[C \cup U]$ is represented by the string $a_1 a_2 \cdots a_n$. An *equation* is $w_1 = w_2$ where w_1 and w_2 are words of $F[C \cup U]$.

　　A *monoid substitution* σ for $F[C \cup U]$ is a function from U to the set of words of $F[C \cup U]$. If w is a word of $F[C \cup U]$ then $w\sigma$ is formed by simultaneously replacing each occurrence of each unknown x in w by $x\sigma$.

　　The monoid problem is defined as follows.

Definition 4.95 Let $\{w_1 = v_1, \ldots, w_n = v_n\}$ be a set of equations whose left and right sides are words of a monoid $F[C \cup U]$.

　　The *monoid problem* is to decide whether or not there exists a monoid substitution σ for $F[C \cup U]$ such that $w_i\sigma$ is identical to $v_i\sigma$ where $1 \leq i \leq n$.

　　There is a strong similarity between the monoid problem and second-order monadic unification. This is made precise by reducing second-order monadic unification to the monoid problem.

Theorem 4.96 *The second-order monadic unification problem reduces to the monoid problem.*

　　A recent proof of the theorem is presented by Farmer [53]. Makanin showed that the monoid problem is decidable [127]. This well-known problem was open for twenty-five years [9].

　　The significance of the Theorem 4.96 is now immediate.

Corollary 4.97 *Second-order monadic unification is decidable.*

　　Farmer has extended this result by showing that variables need not be monadic [53].

---

[9]Siekmann [175] notes that the monoid problem has also been called Löb's problem, Markov's problem, and the Stringunification problem.

Theorem 4.98 *(Farmer.) Every second-order unification problem*

$$\{\langle s_1, t_1 \rangle, \ldots, \langle s_n, t_n \rangle\}$$

is decidable provided that $|\tau(c)| \leq 1$ *for every constant symbol* c *occurring in* s_i *and* t_i *where* $1 \leq i \leq n$.

Plotkin [156] gave the first associative unification procedure, related it to the monoid problem, showed that there could be an infinite set of unifiers, and conjectured that the problem is decidable. Siekmann [174] showed that this procedure produces a sound, complete, and minimal set of unifiers (CSMU).

Huet, and Winterstein [195] derived second-order monadic unification procedures from Huet's procedure for higher-order unification [97], a version of which was presented in Section 4.2. Winterstein's procedure is limited to initial disagreement sets which are singletons, and it does not always terminate [53]. Farmer has apparently derived a sound, complete, and terminating procedure for second-order monadic unification from Huet's procedure for higher-order unification [53].

4.6 First-Order Equational Unification

In general, first-order equational unification and matching is recursively undecidable because Hilbert's Tenth Problem can be reduced to these problems [22, 85]. Sometimes a complete set of minimal E-unifiers does not exist [102], and a disagreement set can have an infinite set of unifiers [156].

A survey of first-order E-unification was presented by Siekmann [176]. There is a procedure for enumerating a complete set of first-order E-unifiers for every finite set of first--order equations [66], and an improved version of it which has less non-determinism [46]. First-order E-unification is currently used in theorem proving [65] for example, and to manipulate hardware descriptions and verify hardware by using unification in Boolean algebras [23, 131].

First-order unification is a special case of first-order E-unification. The first-order unifiers of a disagreement set can be partially ordered by the relation $\leq$ where $\sigma \leq \rho$ if and only if there is a substitution θ such that $\sigma\theta$ is ρ. A most general unifier of a disagreement set is a least upper bound of the unifiers of the set under this ordering [101]. From a category-theoretic viewpoint, Rydeheard and Burstall [169] present a unification algorithm based on an observation by Goguen [75] that a most general unifier is a coequalizer in a Kleisli category [120].

Terms can also be partially ordered by the relation $\leq$ where $s \leq t$ for terms s and t if and only if there is a substitution θ such that $s\theta$ is t. Using this ordering, Plotkin [154] observed that when two terms are unifiable, they have a least upper bound in this ordering which is their most general common instance. The greatest lower bound of any two terms using this ordering is their least general generalization which always exists [155].

There are linear time sequential unification algorithms [15, 148], and efficient algorithms for implementations [130]. Dwork et al. [50] show that unification is log-space complete for $\mathcal{P}$. Vitter and Simons [192] show that despite this result, the time for a sequential random access machine to solve a unification problem can be sped-up by more than a constant factor by using a concurrent-read, concurrent-write parallel random access machine with a polynomial number of processors. Wolfram [198] shows that the number of maximal unifiable and minimal nonunifiable subsets of a unification problem can increase exponentially, and whether or not there is such a subset whose size exceeds a given bound is a NP-complete problem. These intractability results apply to all forms of higher-order equational unification.

In the next chapter, we define higher-order resolution using higher-order equational unification.

Chapter 5

Higher-Order Equational Logic Programming

Using higher-order equational unification, we now generalize the resolution principle [166] to normal form CTT formulas, and prove a Higher-Order Resolution Theorem.

We then define CTT Horn clauses and show that they meet the programming language criteria of Section 1.2 by being computationally adequate, and by possessing unique least model semantics. Validity in the general sense for CTT Horn clauses can be determined from a single general model. These results are then combined with the Higher-Order Resolution Theorem.

We also define the operational semantics of CTT programs, and show using fixed point methods its coincidence with the model-theoretic semantics presented earlier in Sections 3.5 and 3.6.

5.1 Higher-Order Equational Resolution

We begin by defining the clause form of a closed normal form CTT formula. It is similar to the clause form of first-order formulas in Skolem normal form which we discussed in Section 1.1.5.

Definition 5.1 By Definition 3.32, every closed normal form CTT formula t has the form

$$\Pi(\lambda x_1.\Pi(\lambda x_2.\cdots\Pi(\lambda x_n.(r_1 \wedge \cdots \wedge r_m)\cdots)))$$

where $r_1 \wedge \cdots \wedge r_m$ is in conjunctive normal form, $n \geq 0$, $m \geq 1$, and each r_i has the form $(s_{i,1} \vee \cdots \vee s_{i,n_i})$ and $1 \leq i \leq m$.

The *clause form* of t is the set $\{\{s_{1,1},\ldots,s_{1,n_1}\},\ldots,\{s_{m,1},\ldots,s_{m,n_m}\}\}$

A finite set of literals is a *CTT clause* if and only if the head of each positive literal in the set is not a variable, and for each negative literal in the set of the form $\neg t$, the head of t is a not a variable.

Definition 5.2 If t is the set $\{\{s_{1,1},\ldots,s_{1,n_1}\},\ldots,\{s_{m,1},\ldots,s_{m,n_m}\}\}$ where the $s_{i,j}$ are CTT formulas over $\mathcal{S} - \{\Pi\}$, then this abbreviates the formula:

$$\Pi(\lambda x_1.\Pi(\lambda x_2.\cdots\Pi(\lambda x_k.((s_{1,1} \vee \cdots \vee s_{1,n_1}) \wedge \cdots \wedge (s_{m,1} \vee \cdots \vee s_{m,n_m})))))$$

where $\{x_1, \ldots, x_k\} = \bigcup_{1 \le i \le m, 1 \le j \le n_i} \mathcal{F}(s_{i,j})$.

The *normal form of t* is the clause form of the normal form of the above formula.

Definition 5.3 A pair of literals is a *mixed pair* if and only if one of them is a positive literal and the other is a negative literal.

Remark 5.4 Throughout this chapter, where it is not stated explicitly, the following assumptions are made.

- The signature $\mathcal{S}$ is a CTT signature, (Definition 3.21).

- All terms are CTT terms over $\mathcal{S}$, (Definition 3.8).

- All general models are general models over $\mathcal{S}$, (Definition 3.13), and the assumption in Remark 3.34 applies to the denotations of parameters.

- The range of all substitutions is the set of CTT terms over $\mathcal{S}$, and all substitutions are $\beta\bar{\eta}$-normalized substitutions, (Definition 2.41, and Definition 2.48).

- E is an equational theory over $\mathcal{S}$, and the matrix of each equation in E is a literal, (Definition 4.1, Notation 4.2, and Definitions 3.26 and 3.29).

- A relation $\sim$ is a term relation on closed terms over $\mathcal{S}$, (Definition 3.46), where $s \sim t$ if and only if $E \vdash s = t$.

- $\mathcal{T}_E$ enumerates a sound and complete set of E-unifiers, (Definition 4.22).

We shall consider higher-order resolution for closed clauses first, and then the general case.

Definition 5.5 A CTT clause $\{s_1, \ldots, s_n\}$ where $n \ge 0$ is a *closed CTT clause* if and only if $\mathcal{F}(s_i) = \emptyset$ for every $i : 1 \le i \le n$. Every element of a closed clause is a *closed literal*. When $n = 0$, the closed CTT clause is the *empty clause* which is written $\square$.

Analogously to first-order resolution as discussed in Section 1.1.3, we define a higher-order Herbrand universe, and the saturation of CTT clauses over subsets of this universe.

Definition 5.6 The *CTT universe* $\mathcal{S}_\mathcal{U}$ is the set of all CTT terms over $\mathcal{S} - \{\Pi\}$. Let the set

$$R = \{\{s_{1,1}, \ldots, s_{1,n_1}\}, \ldots\}$$

be a possibly infinite set of CTT clauses, $V = \bigcup_{1 \le i, 1 \le j \le n_i} \mathcal{F}(s_{i,j})$, and $\mathcal{P}_\mathcal{U} \subseteq \mathcal{S}_\mathcal{U}$.

The *saturation* $\mathcal{P}_\mathcal{U}(R)$ of R is a set each of whose elements is the normal form of $\{s_{i,1}\theta, \ldots, s_{i,n_i}\theta\}$ for every $i \ge 1$ and $\theta : V \to \mathcal{P}_\mathcal{U}$.

5.1.1 $\sim$-λ-Models and Closed Resolution

We shall define an unsatisfiability procedure using a higher-order form of ground resolution.

We recall from Corollary 3.58 that a $\sim$-λ-model is uniquely determined by specifying the closed literals which have the denotation T in the model.

Definition 5.7 The set $\mathcal{M}_\sim$ is the set of all closed literals each of whose denotations is T in a $\sim$-λ-model.

Notation 5.8 We shall sometimes use $\mathcal{M}_\sim$ in any context where the $\sim$-λ-model that it abbreviates would have been used.

We have the following correspondences of $\mathcal{M}_\sim$, validity of a closed CTT formula in $\mathcal{M}_\sim$, and satisfiability of a CTT formula in $\mathcal{M}_\sim$.

Lemma 5.9 *Let the formula t be a closed normal form CTT formula over a signature $S - \{\Pi\}$, and S be its CTT clause form. Then $\mathcal{M}_\sim \models t$ if and only if every clause in S contains a literal in $\mathcal{M}_\sim$.*

Proof: By Definition 5.1, S is a closed clause. The result follows by Definition 3.10 of the denotations of the logical constants, and Definition 3.13 of a general model. $\square$

Corollary 5.10 *Every set of CTT clauses containing $\square$ is unsatisfiable in every general $\sim$-model.*

We shall now generalize ground resolution to the higher-order case. Initially, we shall use higher-order equational unification rather than an axiomatization of equality. Plotkin observed that in first-order resolution, equational unification can make searching for refutations more efficient than using standard unification with explicit equality theories [156]. This observation should also hold for CTT clauses.

Definition 5.11 Let C_1 and C_2 be two closed CTT clauses which have mixed pair of literals $s \in C_1$ and $\neg t \in C_2$.

The CTT clause $(C_1 - \{s\}) \cup (C_2 - \{\neg t\})$ is a *closed CTT resolvent* of C_1 and C_2 if and only if $\mathcal{T}_E\{\langle s, t \rangle\}$ is not $\emptyset$.

A closed CTT resolvent maintains the basic property of closed resolvents in first-order resolution.

Lemma 5.12 *Let C_1 and C_2 be two closed CTT clauses and $(s, \neg t)$ be a mixed pair of literals where $s \in C_1$ and $\neg t \in C_2$, and M be a general $\sim$-model. If C_1 and C_2 have a closed CTT resolvent $(C_1 - \{s\}) \cup (C_2 - \{\neg t\})$ and $M \models_\sim C_1$ and $M \models_\sim C_2$ then $M \models_\sim (C_1 - \{s\}) \cup (C_2 - \{\neg t\})$.*

Proof: By the last assumption of Remark 5.4 it follows from Theorem 4.23 that $\mathcal{T}_E$ has the Logical Soundness property of Definition 4.19. Since $\mathcal{T}_E\{\langle s, t\rangle\} \neq \emptyset$, we have that the denotations of s and t are the same in $\mathcal{M}$. Therefore, one of the denotations in $\mathcal{M}$ of s or $\neg t$ is F. It follows that the denotation of at least one of the literals in $(C_1 - \{s\}) \cup (C_2 - \{\neg t\})$ in $\mathcal{M}$ is T. By Theorem 5.9 and Theorem 3.52, we have $\mathcal{M} \models_\sim (C_1 - \{s\}) \cup (C_2 - \{\neg t\})$.
□

Definition 5.13 If S is any set of closed CTT clauses, then the *closed CTT resolution* $\mathcal{R}_\sim(S)$ consists of every clause in S and every closed resolvent of every pair of clauses in S using $\mathcal{T}_E$.

Definition 5.14 The set $\mathcal{R}_\sim^n(S)$ where $n \geq 0$ is

- $\mathcal{R}_\sim^0(S) = S$.

- $\mathcal{R}_\sim^{k+1}(S) = \mathcal{R}_\sim(\mathcal{R}_\sim^k(S))$ where $k \geq 0$.

For every set S of closed clauses, and every term relation $\sim$ there is a number $m \geq 0$ such that $\mathcal{R}_\sim^{m+1}(S) = \mathcal{R}_\sim^m(S)$. If $\mathcal{R}_\sim^m(S)$ contains □ we can conclude that S is unsatisfiable in every general $\sim$-model. This observation leads us to the Closed Resolution Theorem.

Theorem 5.15 *(Closed Resolution Theorem.) Let S be any finite set of closed CTT clauses. Then S is unsatisfiable in every general $\sim$-model if and only if there is $m \geq 0$ such that $\square \in \mathcal{R}_\sim^m(S)$.*

Proof: If $\square \in \mathcal{R}_\sim^m(S)$ the result follows by Corollary 5.10, Lemma 5.12, and induction on m. To show the converse, if $\mathcal{R}_\sim^m(S)$ does not contain □ and S is unsatisfiable in every general $\sim$-model, then a contradiction can be formed by constructing a $\sim$-λ-model for S in an analogous way to the construction for ground resolution [166]. □

5.1.2   The General Level

We now consider forming resolvents of CTT clauses whose literals may contain free variables, before giving our Higher-Order Resolution Theorem.

Definition 5.16 Let C_1 and C_2 be CTT clauses, and μ be a renaming substitution such that $\mathcal{F}(C_1\mu) \cap \mathcal{F}(C_2\mu) = \emptyset$. Let $s \in C_1\mu$, $\neg t \in C_2\mu$, and $W = \{\langle s, t\rangle\}$ where $(s, \neg t)$ is a mixed pair of literals.
    A *CTT resolvent* of S and T is the normal form of $((C_1\mu - \{s\}) \cup (C_2\mu - \{\neg t\}))\theta$ where $\theta \in \mathcal{T}_E W \neq \emptyset$.

The sets $\mathcal{R}_\sim(S)$, $\mathcal{R}_\sim^n(S)$ are defined in the analogous way to their closed counterparts in Definitions 5.13 and 5.14, respectively. Two CTT clauses can have an infinitely many resolvents because $\mathcal{T}_E W$ may not be finite. The next lemma leads directly to the Higher--Order Resolution Theorem.

Lemma 5.17 *Let S be a set of CTT clauses, and $\mathcal{P}_\mathcal{U} \subseteq \mathcal{S}_\mathcal{U}$. Then*

$$\mathcal{R}_\sim(\mathcal{P}_\mathcal{U}(S)) \subseteq \mathcal{P}_\mathcal{U}(\mathcal{R}_\sim(S)).$$

Proof: The proof is similar to that for first-order resolution [166]. If $C \in \mathcal{R}_\sim(\mathcal{P}_\mathcal{U}(S))$ and $C \in \mathcal{P}_\mathcal{U}(S)$, then $C \in \mathcal{P}_\mathcal{U}(\mathcal{R}_\sim(S))$ because $S \subseteq \mathcal{R}_\sim(S)$ by Definition 5.13.

Otherwise, C is the closed resolvent of two closed clauses C_1' and C_2' which are the normal forms of $C_1\mu\theta_1$ and $C_2\mu\theta_2$ respectively, where $C_1, C_2 \in S$, μ is a renaming substitution which renames them apart, and $\theta_1 : \mathcal{F}(C_1\mu) \rightarrow \mathcal{P}_\mathcal{U}$ and $\theta_2 : \mathcal{F}(C_2\mu) \rightarrow \mathcal{P}_\mathcal{U}$ are substitutions.

By Definition 5.11 of closed CTT resolvent, there are literals $s \in C_1'$ and $\neg t \in C_2'$ such that $(s, \neg t)$ is a mixed pair of literals and $\mathcal{T}_E\{\langle s, t \rangle\}$ is not $\emptyset$, and $C = (C_1' - \{s\}) \cup (C_2' - \{\neg t\})$.

By Definition 5.1 of CTT clause, there are literals $s_1 \in C_1\mu$ and $\neg t_1 \in C_2\mu$ such that the normal form of $s_1\mu\theta_1$ is s, and the normal form of $\neg t_1\mu\theta_2$ is $\neg t$. The substitution $\theta = \theta_1\theta_2$ is an E-unifier of $\{\langle s_1\mu, t_1\mu \rangle\}$. By the completeness property of $\mathcal{T}_E$ which we assumed in Remark 5.4, there are substitutions σ and ρ such that $\sigma\rho = \theta$ and $\sigma \in \mathcal{T}_E\{\langle s_1\mu, t_1\mu \rangle\}$.

Hence, by Definition 5.16 of CTT resolvent, the normal form C_3 of $((C_1 - \{s_1\}) \cup (C_2 - \{\neg t_1\}))\mu\sigma$ is a resolvent of C_1 and C_2. It follows that the normal form of $C_3\rho$ is C. Therefore $C \in \mathcal{P}_\mathcal{U}(\mathcal{R}_\sim(S))$, as required. $\square$

Corollary 5.18 *Let S be a set of CTT clauses and $\mathcal{P}_\mathcal{U} \subseteq \mathcal{S}_\mathcal{U}$. Then*

$$\mathcal{R}_\sim^m(\mathcal{P}_\mathcal{U}(S)) \subseteq \mathcal{P}_\mathcal{H}(\mathcal{R}_\sim^m(S)).$$

Proof: The proof is by induction on m. It is analogous to the proof for first-order resolution and it uses Lemma 5.17 in the same way. $\square$

We can now prove our Higher-Order Resolution Theorem.

Theorem 5.19 *Let S be any finite set of CTT clauses. Then S is unsatisfiable in every general $\sim$-model if and only if $\square \in \mathcal{R}_\sim^m(S)$ for some $m \geq 0$.*

Proof: S is unsatisfiable in every general $\sim$-model over $\mathcal{S}$ if and only if for some $\mathcal{P}_\mathcal{U} \subseteq \mathcal{S}_\mathcal{U}$ and some $m \geq 0$, $\square \in \mathcal{R}_\sim^m(\mathcal{P}_\mathcal{U}(S))$, by the Closed Resolution Theorem (Theorem 5.15) and the Higher-Order Skolem-Herbrand-Gödel Theorem (Theorem 3.59).

By Corollary 5.18, this holds if and only if $\square \in \mathcal{P}_\mathcal{U}(\mathcal{R}_\sim^m(S))$. The result follows from the observation that $\square \in \mathcal{P}_\mathcal{U}(\mathcal{R}_\sim^m(S))$ if and only if $\square \in \mathcal{R}_\sim^m(S)$. $\square$

Remark 5.20 It is not essential to build an equality theory in to the higher-order unification procedure, as happens with $\mathcal{T}_E$ or special forms of it [163, 180]. We could instead use higher-order pre-unification as described in Section 4.2, and have additional clauses for the CTT equality theory E, and for the axioms of the reflexivity, symmetry, transitivity, and substitutivity of equality. Another possibility is to use linear paramodulation [24, 167] generalized to CTT clauses.

5.2   CTT and Logic Programming

We now define a higher-order logic programming language based on CTT Horn clauses.

Definition 5.21 CTT as a programming language consists of sets of clauses of these forms:

- A *CTT definite clause* is a CTT clause of the form

$$\{A_1, \neg A_2, \ldots, \neg A_n\}$$

  where A_1 is the only positive literal in the clause, and $n \geq 0$.

- If $n = 0$, the CTT definite clause is the empty clause, $\square$.

- A *CTT goal clause* is a CTT clause of the form

$$\{\neg A_2, \ldots, \neg A_n\}.$$

- A *CTT Horn clause* is either a CTT definite clause or a CTT goal clause.

- A *CTT program* is a finite set of CTT definite clauses.

Remark 5.22 In addition to the assumptions made in Remark 5.4 above, we also use the following notations.

- P is a CTT program.

- G, possibly occurring with an integer subscript, is a CTT goal.

At the first-order level, this definition subsumes logic programming [52], logic programming with equality and equational unification [45, 93], and their many-sorted versions. It immediately follows that CTT Horn clauses are computationally adequate: they can compute any Turing computable function since this property holds for first-order Horn clauses [189], as discussed in Section 1.2.3.

Notation 5.23 Using logic programming notation, we abbreviate

- a CTT definite clause $\{A_1, \neg A_2, \ldots, \neg A_n\}$ by $A_1 : - A_2, \ldots, A_n.$,

- a CTT goal clause $\{\neg G_1, \ldots, \neg G_n\}$ by $: - G_1, \ldots, G_n.$, and

- a binder $\lambda x.$ by \X..

We write parameters in lower case letters, and variables in upper case letters in CTT programs.

Example 5.24 CTT logic programs allow functional and relational computations to be separated. The resulting programs are often more concise than their relational counterparts.

We could write the following program, with clauses for **append**, for finding all of the effects of permutations on a finite list.

```
perm(nil, nil).
perm(L, cons(H, T)) :- append(V, cons(H, U), L),
                       append(V, U, W),
                       perm(W, T).
```

Instead, it is possible to write the following program with suitable types for its primitive symbols.

```
perm(nil, nil).
perm(app(V, cons(H, U)), cons(H, T)) :- perm(app(V, U), T).

app(nil, L) = L.
app(cons(H, T), L) = cons(H, app(T, L)).
```

The term \L.\M.perm(L, M) can then be used in goals and program clauses. ○

Example 5.25 The previous example expressed **app** equationally. Many other functions on lists can be expressed in this way, and it is possible to encode directly much of the Bird-Meertens Formalism [18] as CTT equations or conditional equations with suitable types. The functions defined can then be used in other CTT logic program clauses, and CTT predicates can be used as the arguments of these functions.

Here are the clauses for **map** and **reduce**.

```
map(F, nil) = nil.
map(F, cons(A, nil)) = cons((F A), nil).
map(F, app(X, Y)) = app(map(F, X), map(F, Y)).

reduce(OP, OP_id, nil) = OP_id.
reduce(OP, OP_id, cons(A, nil)) = A.
reduce(OP, OP_id, app(X, Y)) = OP(reduce(OP, OP_id, X),
                                  reduce(OP, OP_id, Y)).
```

A function defined by cases can also be expressed by using conditional equations of the form:

```
h(X) = f(X) :- p(X).
h(X) = g(X) :- q(X).
```

○

In Section 1.2.1, we considered the existence of a unique least model for a first-order logic program to be a necessary condition for Horn clause logic to be regarded as a programming language. We now show that this criterion is also met by CTT programs.

5.2.1   Least CTT Models

We now define the intersection of two λ-models. This will be used to define least λ-models for CTT Horn clauses.

Definition 5.26 Let M and N be λ-models over a CTT signature S. The *intersection* $M \cap N$ of M and N is a λ-model. By Corollary 3.58, it is uniquely defined by specifying the set of all closed literals over S which have the denotation T in the model: for every closed literal s, we have $\mathcal{V}^{M \cap N} s$ is T if and only if $\mathcal{V}^M s$ is T and $\mathcal{V}^N s$ is T.

We also define the intersection of term relations.

Definition 5.27 Let $\sim_1$ and $\sim_2$ be two term relations on closed terms over a signature S. Their *intersection*, which is denoted by $\sim_1 \cap \sim_2$, is the intersection of their representations as sets of ordered pairs.

We will use Definition 5.27 in the next theorem.

Theorem 5.28 *If M is a $\sim_1$-λ-model over S and N is a $\sim_2$-λ-model over S, then their intersection $M \cap N$ is a $\sim_1 \cap \sim_2$-λ-model.*

Proof: Let s and t be any closed terms over S such that $s \sim_1 \cap \sim_2 t$. From Definition 5.26 and Definition 5.27, we have $\mathcal{V}^{M \cap N}(s = t)$.
     Therefore, $M \cap N$ is a $\sim_1 \cap \sim_2$-λ-model, as required. $\square$

From Theorem 5.28, we obtain the following basic result for characterizing least CTT models.

Theorem 5.29 *Let S be a finite set of CTT Horn clauses. If M is a $\sim_1$-λ-model and N is a $\sim_2$-λ-model, $M \models_{\sim_1} S$ and $N \models_{\sim_2} S$, then $M \cap N \models_{\sim_1 \cap \sim_2} S$.*

Proof: Suppose on the contrary, that $M \cap N \models_{\sim_1 \cap \sim_2} S$ does not hold. By the higher-order Skolem-Herbrand-Gödel Theorem (Theorem 3.59), there is a CTT clause C in S which is either

- a CTT definite clause $\{A_1, \neg A_2, \ldots, \neg A_n\}$, or

- a CTT goal clause $\{\neg A_1, \ldots, \neg A_n\}$

and a substitution $\theta : \mathcal{X} \to S_u$ such that $M \cap N \models_{\sim_1 \cap \sim_2} C\theta$ does not hold.
     If C is a CTT definite clause, then the denotations of $A_2\theta, \ldots, A_n\theta$ in $M \cap N$ are all T. Therefore, by Definition 5.26, their denotations in M, and in N must also be T. Since we have assumed $M \models_{\sim_1} S$ and $N \models_{\sim_2} S$ it follows that the denotations of $A_1\theta$ in N and N are T. But then, by Definition 5.26 the denotation of $A_1\theta$ in $M \cap N$ must also be T, so that we have reached the contradiction that $M \cap N \models_{\sim_1 \cap \sim_2} C\theta$ holds.
     If C is a CTT goal clause, the result is shown in a similar way. $\square$

Corollary 5.30 *Let S be a finite set of CTT Horn clauses. The set of all λ-models in which S is valid is a complete lattice under the ordering $\leq$ where for any two such models $\mathcal{M}$ and $\mathcal{N}$, we have $\mathcal{M} \leq \mathcal{N}$ if and only if $\mathcal{M} \cap \mathcal{N}$ is $\mathcal{M}$.*

The existence of a unique least λ-model is a direct consequence of this observation. It implies that CTT programs meet the programming language criterion of having a unique model. Unlike the first-order case without equality theories [52], there are families of least models indexed by term relations.

Corollary 5.31 *For every term relation $\sim$ and set of Horn CTT clauses S, there exists a unique least $\sim$-λ-model in which S is valid.*

Notation 5.32 For every set of Horn CTT clauses S, the least $\sim$-λ-model over a CTT signature $\mathcal{S}$ in which S is valid is $\mathcal{M}_\sim(S)$.

Remark 5.33 By Corollary 3.58, to characterize a $\sim$-λ-model over a CTT signature $\mathcal{S}$ it suffices to specify $\sim$, $\mathcal{S}$, and the set of all closed literals whose denotation in the model is T. From now on where $\mathcal{S}$ is fixed, we shall identify $\sim$-λ-models, and $\mathcal{M}_\sim(S)$ in particular, with such sets of closed literals, and refer to them as $\sim$-λ-models.

We now combine Corollary 5.31 with our Higher-Order Resolution Theorem (Theorem 5.19) to obtain the following theorem.

Theorem 5.34 *Let $\sim$ be a term relation for closed terms over a CTT signature $\mathcal{S}$, P be a CTT program over $\mathcal{S}$ and G be a CTT goal clause over $\mathcal{S}$. The following statements are equivalent:*

- *There is $n \geq 0$ such that $\square \in \mathcal{R}_\sim^n(P \cup \{G\})$.*

- *$P \cup \{G\}$ is unsatisfiable in every general $\sim$-model over $\mathcal{S}$.*

- *$P \cup \{G\}$ is unsatisfiable in every $\sim$-λ-model over $\mathcal{S}$.*

- *$P \cup \{G\}$ is unsatisfiable in $\mathcal{M}_\sim(P)$.*

- *$\mathcal{M}_\sim(P) \models_\sim \neg G$.*

- *$P \models_\sim \neg G$.*

- *$\mathcal{M}_\sim(P) \models_\sim P \supset \neg G$.*

- *$\models_\sim P \supset \neg G$.*

We now consider the operational semantics of CTT programs and its relation to the model-theoretic semantics we have presented above.

5.2.2   Least Fixed Points

We define the operational semantics of a CTT program and show its coincidence to the declarative or model-theoretic semantics discussed above. To do this we use a fixed point characterization of the least $\sim$-λ-model of a CTT program. Its definition subsumes that for first-order logic programming [52]. The fixed point characterization uses a function $T_{(P,\sim)}$ which is defined using a set of CTT clauses $|P|$.

Definition 5.35 The set $|P|$ is $\mathcal{S}_{\mathcal{U}}(P)$.

Definition 5.36 The *CTT base* $\mathcal{S}_{\mathcal{B}}$ is the set of all CTT formulas over $\mathcal{S}$ whose heads are either $=$ or a parameter.

Here is the definition of $T_{(P,\sim)}$.

Definition 5.37 Let $D \subseteq \mathcal{S}_{\mathcal{B}}$. Then $T_{(P,\sim)}$ is the function $2^{\mathcal{S}_{\mathcal{B}}} \to 2^{\mathcal{S}_{\mathcal{B}}}$ such that

$$T_{(P,\sim)}(D) = \{A \mid (A_0 : - A_1, \ldots, A_n \in |P|) \wedge (\mathcal{F}(A) = \emptyset) \wedge$$
$$T_E\{\langle A, A_0 \rangle, \langle A_1, D_1 \rangle, \ldots, \langle A_n, D_n \rangle\} \neq \emptyset \wedge (D_i \in D) \text{ where } 1 \leq i \leq n\}$$

We now define inductively a set of closed formulas which can characterize a $\sim$-λ- -model for a CTT program. A special case of the definition is equivalent to that for logic programming [52].

Definition 5.38 The *success set* is

$$S_{(P,\sim)} = \cup_{i \geq 0} T^i_{(P,\sim)}(\emptyset)$$

where $T^0_{(P,\sim)}(\emptyset) = \emptyset$, and $T^{k+1}_{(P,\sim)}(\emptyset) = T_{(P,\sim)}(T^k_{(P,\sim)}(\emptyset))$ and $0 \leq k < \omega$.

Kernels are the duals of such inductive definitions [1]. Here is the kernel of the preceding definition which defines another set of closed formulas. It similarly subsumes the version for first-order logic programming [11].

Definition 5.39 The *finite failure set* is

$$F_{(P,\sim)} = \cup_{i \geq 0} F^i_{(P,\sim)}(\emptyset)$$

where $F^0_{(P,\sim)}(\emptyset) = \emptyset$, and $F^{k+1}_{(P,\sim)}(\emptyset) = \mathcal{S}_{\mathcal{B}} - T_{(P,\sim)}(\mathcal{S}_{\mathcal{B}} - F^k_{(P,\sim)}(\emptyset))$ and $0 \leq k < \omega$.

The fixed point characterization of the least $\sim$-λ-model of a CTT program uses classical results of Tarski [190] and Kleene [113], as in the first-order case. These results use monotonic functions on complete lattices.

Proposition 5.40 $T_{(P,\sim)}$ *is a monotonic function on* $2^{\mathcal{S}_{\mathcal{B}}}$: *if* $X \subseteq Y$, *then* $T_{(P,\sim)}(X) \subseteq T_{(P,\sim)}(Y)$ *where* $X, Y \in 2^{\mathcal{S}_{\mathcal{B}}}$.

Proposition 5.41 $(2^{\mathcal{S}_{\mathcal{B}}}, \subseteq)$ *is a complete lattice, with* $\mathcal{S}_{\mathcal{B}}$ *as top element,* $\emptyset$ *as bottom element,* $\cup$ *as join, and* $\cap$ *as meet.*

We shall use the following result [190].

Theorem 5.42 *(Tarski.) Let T be a monotonic function on elements of a complete lattice. Then T has a least fixed point lfp(T), and a greatest fixed point gfp(T).*

Corollary 5.43 *The function $T_{(P,\sim)}$ on the complete lattice $(2^{S_B}, \subseteq)$ has a least fixed point lfp$(T_{(P,\sim)})$ and a greatest fixed point gfp$(T_{(P,\sim)})$.*

Definition 5.44 Let L be a complete lattice and $T : L \to L$ be a mapping.

- $T \uparrow 0$ is the bottom element of L.

- $T \uparrow \omega$ is lub$\{T \uparrow \beta \mid \beta < \omega\}$.

- $T \downarrow 0$ is the top element of L.

- $T \downarrow \omega$ is glb$\{T \downarrow \beta \mid \beta < \omega\}$.

Definition 5.45 A function T on elements of a complete lattice L is a *continuous function* if $T(\text{lub}(X)) = \text{lub}(T(X))$ for every subset X of L all of whose finite subsets have an upper bound in X under the ordering $\subseteq$.

Proposition 5.46 *$T_{(P,\sim)}$ is a continuous function on $(2^{S_B}, \subseteq)$.*

The next theorem is the First Recursion Theorem [113]. It will link the inductive definition of the success set to the fixed point treatment.

Theorem 5.47 *(Kleene.) lfp$(T) = T \uparrow \omega$ where T is a continuous function on elements of a complete lattice.*

As a result, we have:

Corollary 5.48 lfp$(T_{(P,\sim)}) = T_{(P,\sim)} \uparrow \omega$.

The next definition links the finite failure set to the fixed point treatment.

Definition 5.49 $\overline{T_{(P,\sim)} \downarrow \omega} = S_B - (T_{(P,\sim)} \downarrow \omega)$.

We shall define the operational semantics of CTT programs in a way that is closely related to the inductive definitions of Definition 5.38. We use the identification mentioned in Remark 5.33 of $\sim$-λ-models and sets of closed positive literals. To show the coincidence of operational semantics to model-theoretic semantics using the fixed point treatment, we have the following result.

Theorem 5.50 *$\mathcal{M}_\sim(P)$ is the set whose elements are the normal forms of elements of $T_{(P,\sim)} \uparrow \omega$.*

Proof: The proof is a generalization using Lemma 3.33 of the proof for the first-order case without equality [52]. $\square$

Theorem 5.51 *These are identities:*

- $S_{(P,\sim)} = \cup_{i \geq 0} S^i_{(P,\sim)} = \text{lfp}(T_{(P,\sim)}) = T_{(P,\sim)} \uparrow \omega$.

- $F_{(P,\sim)} = \cup_{i \geq 0} F^i_{(P,\sim)} = \overline{T_{(P,\sim)} \downarrow \omega}$.

5.2.3   BF- and SLD-resolution

We define concurrent breadth-first, or BF-resolution for CTT programs, as a generaliz-ation of the first-order case [196]. Its search space is a unique tree called the *BF-tree*.

The definitions of success set (Definition 5.38) and finite failure set (Definition 5.39) correspond to successful and failed BF-searches respectively. We then prove the sound-ness and completeness of BF-search for successful and finitely failed derivations, and the coincidence of operational and model-theoretic semantics.

A *BF-derivation* for a CTT program involves renamed clauses.

Definition 5.52 CTT clauses C_1 and C_2 are *renamed apart* if and only if $\mathcal{F}(C_1) \cap \mathcal{F}(C_2) = \emptyset$.

The following definition of BF-derivation does not involve resolvents: unification prob-lems are recorded in disagreement sets. It suffices to show the existence of an E-unifier for these sets. The goals of a BF-derivation can be mapped to a BF-resolution refutation by instantiating all of them with any such E-unifier and then normalizing them. Before they are normalized, we shall refer to the some of the terms in an instantiated goal as formulas:

Definition 5.53 Let $G =: - G_1, \ldots, G_n$ be a goal clause and θ be a substitution. The *formulas* of $G\theta$ are the n formulas $G_1\theta, \ldots, G_n\theta$.

Definition 5.54 A *BF-derivation* for $P \cup \{G_0\}$, is a sequence $(G_0, W_0), (G_1, W_1), \ldots$ of pairs of goals and disagreement sets which is defined as follows.

Suppose that G_l is : $- A_1, \cdots, A_n$ where $l \geq 0$ and $n \geq 0$. If $l = 0$ then W_0 is $\emptyset$.

- If $n = 0$, the BF-derivation is a *successful derivation of length* l and the set of *answer substitutions* is $\mathcal{T}_E(\cup_{0 \leq i \leq l} W_i)$.

- If $n > 0$, and there is an *input list* I_l of n clauses $H_j : - B_j$ for $1 \leq j \leq n$, which are

  - any n clauses of P renamed apart, and renamed apart from G_k for $0 \leq k \leq l$, and

  - $\mathcal{T}_E(\cup_{0 \leq i \leq l} W_i \cup \{\langle A_1, H_1 \rangle, \ldots, \langle A_n, H_n \rangle\}) \neq \emptyset$

  then, G_{l+1} is the goal clause : $- B_1, \ldots, B_n$, and W_{l+1} is the disagreement set $\{\langle A_1, H_1 \rangle, \ldots, \langle A_n, H_n \rangle\}$.

- Otherwise, the BF-derivation is a *failed derivation of length* l.

A BF-tree represents a search space for a successful derivation.

Definition 5.55 Given $\mathcal{T}_E$, the *BF-tree* for $P \cup \{G_0\}$, where P is a CTT program and G_0 is a goal clause, is defined by:

1. The root of the BF-tree is $(G_0, \emptyset)$.

2. The children of (G_l, W_l) where $l \geq 0$ are all pairs of goal clauses and disagreement sets (G_{l+1}, W_{l+1}) which can be BF-derived from (G_l, W_l) in one step.

Definition 5.56 A *successful branch* or *failed branch* of a BF-tree is a successful or failed BF-derivation, respectively. If every branch of a BF-tree is a failed BF-derivation, then the BF-tree is a *finitely failed BF-tree*.

In Section 1.2, we discussed SLD-resolution, and SLD-trees and fair SLD-trees were described in Section 1.2.4. They have counterparts for Clausal Theory of Types logic programs. BF-derivations seem to be best suited for showing certain soundness and completeness results because they have less non-determinism than SLD-derivations. The latter are preferable for actual implementations because they have more modest space requirements. We shall extend the results for BF-derivations to SLD-derivations in Section 5.2.5 below.

The definitions of SLD-derivation and SLD-tree for a CTT program and goal are similar to Definition 5.54 of BF-derivation and Definition 5.55 of BF-tree, except that each input list contains just one renamed clause from P, and just one literal in each clause of a derivation is selected, rather than every literal.

The definitions of successful and failed branches of a SLD-tree, and a finitely failed SLD-tree follow their BF- forms in Definition 5.56 above. All branches of a BF-tree are fair branches, and a branch in a SLD-tree is a fair branch if whenever a literal occurs in a goal clause G_k of the branch, it is the selected literal of a goal clause G_{k+l} of the branch where $l > 0$. A SLD-tree is a fair SLD-tree if each of its branches is a fair branch.

In a similar way to the first-order case [196], we have the following relations between BF- and SLD-trees.

Theorem 5.57 *Let T_1 and T_2 be BF- or SLD-trees for $P \cup \{G_0\}$.*

- *If T_1 has a successful branch, then so does T_2.*

- *If T_1 has an infinite fair branch, then T_2 has an infinite branch.*

Theorem 5.58 *Let T_1 and T_2 be BF- or SLD-trees for $P \cup \{G_0\}$. If T_1 is finitely failed and T_2 is fair, then T_2 is finitely failed.*

Proof: Suppose that T_2 has a successful or infinite branch. As T_2 is fair, T_1 must have a successful or infinite branch by Theorem 5.57. This is a contradiction, so T_2 must be finitely failed. $\square$

We now show that BF-resolution is sound and complete for success and finite failure. Theorems 5.57 and 5.58 will then be used to show similar results for SLD-resolution in a direct way.

5.2.4   Soundness and Completeness

We now prove that BF-search is sound and complete for success and for finite failure. The following lemma is used in proving the completeness of BF-search for success, and its soundness for finite failure. Since the production of an element of $T^i_{(P,\sim)}(\emptyset)$ (Definition 5.38), or $S_B - F^{i+1}_{(P,\sim)}(\emptyset)$ (Definition 5.39) where $i \geq 0$, is tantamount to a closed BF-derivation, by lifting such a derivation to the form of a BF-derivation, the results can be proved directly.

Notation 5.59 We abbreviate

- $T^l_{(P,\sim)}(\emptyset)$ to S_l,

- $F^{l+1}_{(P,\sim)}(\emptyset)$ to F_l, and

- a CTT definite clause of the form $H : - A_1, \ldots, A_n$ where $n \geq 0$ to $H : - B$, where B is syntactically identical to $A_1, \ldots, A_n$.

- Y_l uniformly stands either for S_l, or for $S_B - F_l$.

Lemma 5.60 *(Lifting Lemma.) If G_0 is the goal clause $: - A_1, \cdots, A_n$ and there is a substitution α_0, such that the formulas of $G_0\alpha_0$ are in Y_l where $l > 0$, then there is a BF--derivation step from $(G_0, \emptyset)$ to (G_1, W_1), and a substitution α_1 such that the formulas of $G_1\mu_0\alpha_1$ are in Y_{l-1} and $\alpha_0\rho_0 = \mu_0\alpha_1$, where $\mu_0 \in \mathcal{T}_E W_1$.*

Proof: By definition of Y_l, there are n closed instances of clauses of P, $H_j\gamma_j : - B_j\gamma_j$ for $1 \leq j \leq n$, where $H_j : - B_j$ is a clause of P and γ_j is a closed substitution, such that $\mathcal{T}_E\{\langle A_1\alpha_0, H_1\gamma_1\rangle, \ldots, \langle A_n\alpha_0, H_n\gamma_n\rangle\} \neq \emptyset$, and when $l > 0$ the formulas of $B_j\gamma_j$ are in Y_{l-1}.

Let $\rho_0 = \gamma_1 \ldots \gamma_n$ and $I = \{H_j : - B_j \mid 1 \leq j \leq n\}$. We can assume that the clauses in I are renamed apart, and each of them is renamed apart from G_0.

This implies that $A_i\alpha_0\rho_0$ is $A_i\alpha_0$, and $H_i\alpha_0\rho_0$ is $H_i\gamma_i$ for every $i : 1 \leq i \leq n$. Therefore, $\mathcal{T}_E\{\langle A_1\alpha_0\rho_0, H_1\alpha_0\rho_0\rangle, \ldots, \langle A_n\alpha_0\rho_0, H_n\alpha_0\rho_0\rangle\} \neq \emptyset$. Since we have assumed in Remark 5.4 that $\mathcal{T}_E$ enumerates a complete set of E-unifiers in accordance with Definition 4.22, there is $\mu_0 \in \mathcal{T}_E W_1$ and a substitution α_1 such that $\alpha_0\rho_0 = \mu_0\alpha_1$.

Hence, by Definition 5.54 of BF-derivation, there is a derivation step from $(G_0, \emptyset)$ to (G_1, W_1) with input list $I_0 = I$, and when $l > 0$, $G_1\mu_0\alpha_1$ is $: - B_1\mu_0\alpha_1, \ldots, B_n\mu_0\alpha_1$ and $\{B_1\mu_0\alpha_1, \ldots, B_n\mu_0\alpha_1\} \subseteq Y_{l-1}$. $\square$

Success Set

Suppose that the formulas of a closed goal clause G_0 are in S_l. They are produced from elements in S_{l-1} which are in turn produced from elements in S_{l-2} and so on. From the definition of $S_{(P,\sim)}$, it is easy to construct a BF-derivation for $P \cup \{G_0\}$.

The following soundness theorem states that all formulas of any closed instance of $G_0\mu$ where μ is an answer substitution for this derivation belong to $S_{(P,\sim)}$.

Theorem 5.61 *If $P \cup \{G_0\}$ has a successful BF-derivation of length l, then the formulas of any closed instance $G_0\mu\alpha$ of $G_0\mu$ are in S_l, where μ is any answer substitution of the derivation.*

Proof: Since we have assumed in Remark 5.4 that $\mathcal{T}_E$ enumerates a sound set of E-unifiers in accordance with Definition 4.22, every answer substitution μ of the BF-derivation is an E-unifier of W_l.

Apply $\mu\alpha$ to all the goal clauses of the derivation and apply any substitution so that all formulas are closed. By Definition 5.54 of BF-derivation, and Definition 5.38 of $S_{(P,\sim)}$, if all formulas of the instantiated goal clause G_n are in S_{i-1}, then all formulas of G_{n-1} are in S_i.

As G_l is the empty goal clause, its formulas are in $\emptyset = S_0$. $\square$

The following theorem states the completeness of BF-search.

Theorem 5.62 *If there is a substitution α_0 such that the formulas of $G_0\alpha_0$ are in S_l for a least $l > 0$, then $P \cup \{G_0\}$ has a successful BF-derivation of length l such that $G_0\alpha_0 = G_0\mu\gamma$, for an answer substitution μ and a substitution γ.*

Proof: Since the formulas of $G_0\alpha_0 \in S_l$, by the leastness of l, after l repeated applications of the Lifting Lemma (Lemma 5.60), there are l BF-derivation steps from $(G_0, \emptyset)$ to (G_l, W_l) and substitutions α_j such that the formulas of $G_j\mu_0 \cdots \mu_{j-1}\alpha_j$ are in S_{l-j} for $0 \le j \le l$.

From the Lifting Lemma, we have that $\alpha_i\rho_i = \mu_i\alpha_{i+1}$ where $1 \le i < k$. Therefore, $\alpha_i\rho_i\rho_{i+1} = \mu_i\alpha_{i+1}\rho_{i+1}$, and $\mu_i\alpha_{i+1}\rho_{i+1} = \mu_i\mu_{i+1}\alpha_{i+2}$. It follows that $G_0\alpha_0 = G_0\alpha_0\rho_0 \cdots \rho_{k-1}$ and $G_0\alpha_0\rho_0 \cdots \rho_{k-1} = G_0\mu_0 \cdots \mu_{k-1}\alpha_k$. The substitution $\mu = \mu_0 \cdots \mu_{k-1}$ is an answer substitution, and $\gamma = \alpha_k$, as required. $\square$

Finite Failure Set

The following theorem states the soundness of BF-search for finite failure.

Theorem 5.63 *If every BF-derivation for $P \cup \{G_0\}$ is failed by length $\le l$, then every closed instance of G_0 contains a formula in F_l.*

Proof: The proof is by induction on l. If every BF-derivation for $P \cup \{G_0\}$ is failed by length zero, then by definition of F_0 every closed instance of G_0 contains a formula in F_0.

The induction hypothesis is that the theorem is true for all BF-derivations of length $l - 1$. If every BF-derivation for G_0 is failed by length $\le l$ then, by the induction hypothesis, every closed instance of every G_1 contains a formula in F_{l-1}. Suppose there is a substitution α_0 such that the formulas of $G_0\alpha_0$ are in $S_B - F_l$. Then by the Lifting Lemma, there is a BF-derivation step from $(G_0, \emptyset)$ to (G_1, W_1) and a substitution α_1 such that the formulas of $G_1\mu_0\alpha_1$ are in $S_B - F_{l-1}$. This is a contradiction. Therefore every closed instance of G_0 contains a formula in F_l. $\square$

The next theorem states that BF-search is complete for finite failure.

Theorem 5.64 *If every closed instance of G_0 contains a formula in F_l, then every BF--derivation for $P \cup \{G_0\}$ is failed by length $\leq l$.*

Proof: The proof is by induction on l. If every closed instance of G_0 contains a formula in F_0, then every BF-derivation for $P \cup \{G_0\}$ is failed by length zero. Otherwise, by the definitions of BF-derivation and F_0, a closed instance of G_0 could be found which does not contain a formula in F_0.

The induction hypothesis is that the theorem is true for all BF-derivations of length $l - 1$. Let every closed instance of G_0 contain a formula in $S_B - F_l$. If there is a descendant (G_1, W_1) of $(G_0, \emptyset)$ and a substitution β such that the formulas of $G_1 \mu_0 \beta$ are in $S_B - F_{l-1}$, by the definitions of BF-derivation and F_l, the formulas of a closed instance of $G_0 \mu_0 \beta$ are in $S_B - F_l$ where $\mu_0 \in T_E W_1$.

This is a contradiction. Hence every closed instance of every descendant goal clause G_1 contains a formula in F_{l-1} and by the induction hypothesis, every BF-derivation for $P \cup \{G_0\}$ is failed by length $\leq l$. $\square$

5.2.5   Declarative and Operational Semantics

We can now combine Theorem 5.34 and Theorem 5.51 for declarative semantics of CTT programs with Theorem 5.61, and Theorem 5.62 of the soundness and completeness of BF-search to show their coincidence. This coincidence is extended to SLD-search by using Theorems 5.57 and 5.58.

Theorem 5.65 *The following statements are equivalent.*

- *$P \cup \{G_0\}$ is unsatisfiable in every general $\sim$-model.*

- *$P \cup \{G_0\}$ is unsatisfiable in every $\sim$-λ-model.*

- *$P \cup \{G_0\}$ is unsatisfiable in $\mathcal{M}_\sim(P)$.*

- *There is a substitution α such that the formulas of $G_0 \alpha$ are in $S_{(P, \sim)}$.*

- *There is a least $l > 0$ such that the formulas of $G_0 \alpha$ are in S_l.*

- *The BF-tree for $P \cup \{G_0\}$ has a successful branch of length l with answer substitution μ, and there is a substitution β such that $G_0 \alpha$ is $G_0 \mu \beta$.*

- *There is a SLD-tree for $P \cup \{G_0\}$ which has a successful branch with answer substitution μ, and there is a substitution β such that $G_0 \alpha$ is $G_0 \mu \beta$.*

- *Every SLD-tree for $P \cup \{G_0\}$ has a successful branch with answer substitution μ, and there is a substitution β such that $G_0 \alpha$ is $G_0 \mu \beta$.*

We can also use Theorem 5.63 and Theorem 5.64 on the soundness and completeness of BF-search for the finite failure set to characterize goals which do not have refutations.

Theorem 5.66 *The following statements are equivalent:*

- *Every closed instance of G_0 contains a formula in $F_{(P,\sim)}$.*

- *There is a least $l > 0$ such that every closed instance of G_0 contains a formula in F_l.*

- *The BF-tree for $P \cup \{G_0\}$ is finitely failed, and the length of none of its branches exceeds l.*

- *There is a finitely failed SLD-tree for $P \cup \{G_0\}$.*

- *Every fair SLD-tree for $P \cup \{G_0\}$ is finitely failed.*

5.3 Discussion

An implementation of a prototype interpreter [200] for first-order equational logic programs is currently being modified for CTT programs. Backtracking is a standard search method, but the interpreter also includes: an optimized form of forward checking with search rearrangement [199], Adaptive Backtracking [197] which is an efficient form of intelligent backtracking which prevents exponential space and time overheads of other methods [198], and iterative-deepening based on the method of Korf [115]. These search methods can be combined.

Some problems, such as those encoded in CTT programs and equational logic programs, require independent searches to be performed for their solution. The methods for the searches can differ. For example, in CTT logic programming the search for unifiers could be done by backtrack search while the search for refutations could be done by breadth-first Adaptive Backtracking.

The prototype interpreter is written in Standard ML [78, 82]. Extensive use is made of ML functors and modules for combining search methods and for combining search methods and example problems. This tool allows comparisons of search methods to be made before an optimized interpreter is designed for CTT programs.

It remains to consider the completeness of our higher-order matching algorithm, and to provide a general procedure for higher-order equational unification. Progress in these areas should increase the efficiency of future implementations, and take the Clausal of Theory of Types beyond this theoretical stage.

Bibliography

[1] P. Aczel, An introduction to inductive definitions, in : Barwise [14], 739–782.

[2] G. Amiot, The undecidability of the second order predicate unification problem, *Archive for Mathematical Logic* **30** (1990) 193–199.

[3] P.B. Andrews, Resolution in type theory, *Journal of Symbolic Logic* **36** (1971) 414–432.

[4] P.B. Andrews, General models, descriptions, and choice in type theory, *Journal of Symbolic Logic* **37** (1972) 385–394.

[5] P.B. Andrews, General models and extensionality, *Journal of Symbolic Logic* **37** (1972) 395–397.

[6] P.B. Andrews, Theorem proving via general matings, *Journal of the Association for Computing Machinery* **28** (1981) 193–214.

[7] P.B. Andrews, *An Introduction to Mathematical Logic and Type Theory: To Truth Through Proof*, Academic, Orlando, 1986.

[8] P.B. Andrews, Connections and higher-order logic, *Proceedings of the Eighth Conference on Automated Deduction*, Lecture Notes in Computer Science **230**, Springer, Berlin, 1986, 1–4.

[9] P.B. Andrews, D. Miller, E.L. Cohen, and F. Pfenning, Automating higher-order logic, in: Bledsoe and Loveland (Eds.) [21], 169–192.

[10] P.B. Andrews, F. Pfenning, S. Issar, and C.P. Klapper, The TPS theorem proving system, *Proceedings of the Eighth Conference on Automated Deduction*, Lecture Notes in Computer Science **230**, Springer, Berlin, 1986, 663–664.

[11] K.R. Apt and M.H. van Emden, Contributions to the theory of logic programming, *Journal of the Association for Computing Machinery* **29** (1982) 841–862.

[12] A. Avron, F. Honsell, I. Mason, and R. Pollack, Using typed lambda calculus to implement formal systems on a machine, Laboratory for Foundations of Computer Science, Department of Computer Science, University of Edinburgh, ECS-LFCS-87-31, July 1987.

[13] M. Baaz and A. Leitsch, Complexity of resolution proofs and function introduction, *Annals of Pure and Applied Logic* **57** (1992) 181–215.

[14] J. Barwise, (Ed.), *Handbook of Mathematical Logic*, North-Holland, Amsterdam, 1977.

[15] L.D. Baxter, A practically linear unification algorithm, Research Report, CS–76–13 (February 1976), University of Waterloo, Waterloo, Canada.

[16] G. Bealer and U. Mönnich, Property theories, in: D.M. Gabbay and F. Guenthner (Eds.) [62], (1983) Volume 3, 133–251.

[17] W. Bibel, Computationally improved versions of Herbrand's Theorem, in: Stern, (Ed.) [188], 11–28.

[18] R.S. Bird, Lectures on constructive functional programming, in: *Constructive Methods in Computing Science*, NATO Advanced Study Institutes, Series F, **55**, M. Broy, (Ed.), Springer, Berlin, 1989, 151–216.

[19] G. Birkhoff, On the structure of abstract algebras, *Proceedings of the Cambridge Philosophical Society* (1935) **31** 433–454.

[20] G. Birtwistle and P.A. Subrahmanyam, (Eds.), *VLSI Specification, Verification, and Synthesis*, Kluwer, 1987.

[21] W.W. Bledsoe and D.W. Loveland, (Eds.), *Automated Theorem Proving After 25 Years*, Contemporary Mathematics **29**, American Mathematical Society, Providence, 1984.

[22] A. Bockmayr, A note on a canonical theory with undecidable unification and matching problem, *Journal of Automated Reasoning* **3** (1987) 379–381.

[23] A. Boudet, J-P. Jouannaud, and M. Schmidt-Schauss, Unification in Boolean rings and Abelian groups, *Journal of Symbolic Computation* **8** (1989) 449–477.

[24] C-L. Chang and R.C-T. Lee, *Symbolic Logic and Mechanical Theorem Proving*, Academic, San Diego, 1973.

[25] A. Church, A note on the Entscheidungsproblem, *Journal of Symbolic Logic* **1** (1936), 40–41, 101–102.

[26] A. Church, An unsolvable problem of elementary number theory, *American Journal of Mathematics* **58** (1936) 345–363.

[27] A. Church, A formulation of the Simple Theory of Types, *Journal of Symbolic Logic* **5** (1940) 56–68.

[28] A. Church, *Introduction to Mathematical Logic*, Volume 1, Princeton, 1956.

[29] A. Church and J.B. Rosser, Some properties of conversion, *Transactions of the American Mathematical Society* **39** (1936) 472–482.

[30] L. Chwistek, The theory of constructive types, *Annales de la Société Polonaise de Mathématique* **2** (1924) 9–48; **3** (1925) 92–141.

[31] K.L. Clark, Negation as failure. in : *Logic and Data Bases*. H. Gallaire and J. Minker Eds., Plenum Press, New York, 1978, 293–324.

[32] W.F. Clocksin and C.S. Mellish, *Programming in Prolog*, Third edition, Springer, Berlin, 1987.

[33] A.J. Cohn, A Proof of correctness of the Viper microprocessor: the first level, in: Birtwistle and Subrahmanyam [20].

[34] A. Colmerauer, H. Kanoui, R. Pasero, and P. Roussel, Un système de communication homme-machine en Français, Rapport Preliminaire, Groupe d'Intelligence Artificielle, Université d'Aix-Marseille, Luminy, 1972.

[35] R. Constable et al., *Implementing Mathematics with the Nuprl Proof Development System*, Prentice-Hall, Englewood Cliffs, New Jersey, 1986.

[36] F. Corella, Mechanizing set theory, Research Report RC 14706, International Business Machines Corporation, T.J. Watson Research Center, Yorktown Heights, New York, (June 1989).

[37] T. Coquand and G. Huet, The Calculus of Constructions, *Information and Computation* **76** (1988) 95–120.

[38] B. Courcelle, Fundamental properties of infinite trees, *Theoretical Computer Science* **25** (1983) 95–169.

[39] H.B. Curry and R. Feys, *Combinatory Logic*, Volume I, North-Holland, Amsterdam, 1958.

[40] H.B. Curry, J.R. Hindley, and J.P. Seldin, *Combinatory Logic*, Volume 2, North-Holland, Amsterdam, 1972.

[41] M. Davis, *Computability & Unsolvability*, McGraw-Hill, New York, 1958.

[42] M.D. Davis and H. Putnam, A computing procedure for quantification theory, *Journal of the Association for Computing Machinery* **7** (1960) 210–215.

[43] M. Davis, Eliminating the irrelevant from mechanical proofs, *Proceedings of the Symposium of Applied Mathematics* **18**, American Mathematical Society, Providence, 1963, 15–30.

[44] M. Davis, Why Gödel didn't have Church's Thesis, *Information and Control* **54** (1982) 3–24.

[45] D. DeGroot and G. Lindstrom, (Eds.), *Logic Programming: Functions, Relations and Equations*, Prentice-Hall, Englewood Cliffs, 1986.

[46] D.J. Dougherty and P. Johann, An improved general E-unification procedure, *Journal of Symbolic Computation* **14**, 4 (1992) 303–320.

[47] G. Dowek, L'indécidabilité du filtrage du troisième ordre dans les calculs avec types dépendants ou constructeurs de types, *Compte Rendu à l'Académie des Sciences*, I, 312, 12, 1991.

[48] G. Dowek, Third order matching is decidable, *Proceedings of the Seventh Annual IEEE Symposium on Logic in Computer Science*, IEEE Computer Society, Washington, D.C., 1992, 2–10.

[49] B. Dreben and J. Denton, A supplement to Herbrand, *Journal of Symbolic Logic* **31** (1966) 393–398.

[50] C. Dwork, P.C. Kanellakis, and J.C. Mitchell, On the sequential nature of unification, *Journal of Logic Programming* **1** (1984) 35–50.

[51] C. Elliott and F. Pfenning, A family of program derivations for higher-order unification, Department of Computer Science, Carnegie-Mellon University, Pittsburgh, April 1987.

[52] M.H. van Emden and R.A. Kowalski, The semantics of predicate logic as a programming language, *Journal of the Association for Computing Machinery* **24** (1976) 733–742.

[53] W.M. Farmer, A unification algorithm for second-order monadic terms, *Annals of Pure and Applied Logic* **39** (1988) 131–174.

[54] W.M. Farmer, A partial functions version of Church's Simple Theory of Types, *Journal of Symbolic Logic* **55** (1990) 1269–1291.

[55] W.M. Farmer, Simple second-order languages for which unification is undecidable, *Theoretical Computer Science* **87** (1991) 25–41.

[56] W.M. Farmer, A unification-theoretic method for investigating the k-provability problem, *Annals of Pure and Applied Logic* **51** (1991) 173–214.

[57] W.M. Farmer, J.D. Guttman, and F.J. Thayer, IMPS: system description, *Proceedings of the Eleventh Conference on Automated Deduction*, Lecture Notes in Computer Science, **607**, Springer, Berlin, 1992, 701–705.

[58] A. Felty, Implementing theorem provers in logic programming, Technical Report MS-CIS-87-109, LINC LAB 87, University of Pennsylvania, December 1987.

[59] M. Fitting, *Proof Methods for Modal and Intuitionistic Logics*, Reidel, Dordrecht, 1983.

[60] S. Fortune, D. Leivant, and M. O'Donnell, The expressiveness of simple and second-order type structures, *Journal of the Association for Computing Machinery* **30** (1983) 151–185.

[61] M.P. Fourman, The logic of topoi, in: Barwise [14], 1053–1090.

[62] D.M. Gabbay and F. Guenthner, (Eds.), *Handbook of Philosophical Logic*, **1–4**, Reidel, Dordrecht, 1983.

[63] J.H. Gallier, *Logic for Computer Science*, Harper & Row, New York, 1988.

[64] J.H. Gallier, Unification procedures in automated deduction methods based on matings: a survey, Department of Computer and Information Science, University of Pennsylvania, 1992.

[65] J.H. Gallier, S. Raatz, and W. Snyder, Theorem proving using rigid *E*-unification: equational matings, *Second Annual IEEE Symposium on Logic in Computer Science*, IEEE Computer Society, Washington, D.C., 1987, 338–346.

[66] J.H. Gallier and W. Snyder, Complete sets of transformations for general *E*-unification, *Theoretical Computer Science* **67** (1989) 203–260.

[67] J.H. Gallier and W. Snyder, Designing unification procedures using transformations: a survey, *Proceedings of Logic from Computer Science*, (I. Moskovakis, Ed.), Mathematical Sciences Research Institute, University of California, Berkeley, 1989.

[68] R.O. Gandy, An early proof of normalization by A.M. Turing, in: Hindley and Seldin [90], 453–455.

[69] S.J. Garland and J.V. Guttag, An Overview of LP: The Larch Prover, *Proceedings of the Third International Conference on Rewriting Techniques and Applications*, Lecture Notes in Computer Science **355**, Springer, Berlin, 1989, 137–151.

[70] G. Gentzen, Untersuchungen uber das logische Schliessen, *Mathematische Zeitschrift* (1934) 176–210, 405–431. In: *The Collected Papers of Gerhard Gentzen*, M.E. Szabó, (Ed.), Elsevier North-Holland, New York, 1970, 68–132.

[71] J-Y. Girard, Herbrand's Theorem and proof-theory, in: Stern (Ed.) [188], 29–38.

[72] K. Gödel, Die Vollstandigkeit der Axiome des logischen Funktionenkalküls, *Monatsh. Math. Phys.* **37** (1930) 349–360.

[73] K. Gödel, Über eine bisher noch nicht benütze Erweiterung des finiten Standpunktes, *Dialectica* **12** (1958) 280–287. English translation in: *Journal of Philosophical Logic* **9** (1980) 133–142.

[74] J.A. Goguen and T. Winkler, Introducing OBJ3, Report SRI-CSL-88-9, SRI International, Menlo Park, 1988.

[75] J.A. Goguen, What is unification?: a categorical view of substitution, equation and solution, SRI International, Menlo Park, 1988.

[76] W.D. Goldfarb, The undecidability of the second-order unification problem, *Theoretical Computer Science* **13** (1981) 225–230.

[77] M.J.C. Gordon, HOL: A proof generating system for higher-order logic, in: Birtwistle and Subrahmanyam [20].

[78] M. Gordon, R. Milner, and C.P. Wadsworth, *Edinburgh LCF: A Mechanised Logic of Computation*, Lecture Notes in Computer Science **78**, Springer, Berlin, 1979.

[79] A. Grzegorczyk, Some classes of recursive functions, *Rozprawy Matematyczne* **4** (1953) 46, Instytut Matematyczne Polskiej Akademie Nauk, Warsaw, Poland.

[80] A. Haken, The intractability of resolution, *Theoretical Computer Science* **39** (1985) 297–308.

[81] M. Hanus, Improving control of logic programs by using functional logic languages, *Proceedings of the Fourth International Symposium on Programming Language Implementation and Logic Programming*, Lecture Notes in Computer Science **631**, Springer, Berlin, 1992, 1–23.

[82] R. Harper, R. Milner, and M. Tofte, The definition of Standard ML — Version 3, Technical Report ECS-LFCS-89-81, Department of Computer Science, Edinburgh University, 1989.

[83] R. Harper and R. Pollack, Type checking, universe polymorphism, and typical ambiguity in the Calculus of Constructions, In: J. Diaz and F. Orejas (Eds.), TAPSOFT '89, Proceedings of the International Joint Conference on Theory and Practice of Software Development, Lecture Notes in Computer Science, **352**, volume 2, Springer, Berlin, 1989, 241–258.

[84] J. Van Heijenoort, *From Frege to Gödel: A Source Book in Mathematical Logic, 1879–1931*, Harvard, 1967.

[85] S. Heilbrunner and S. Hölldobler, The undecidability of the unification and matching problem for canonical theories, *Acta Informatica* **24** (1987) 157–171.

[86] P. Henderson, *Functional Programming: Application and Implementation*, Prentice-Hall, London, 1980.

[87] L. Henkin, Completeness in the Theory of Types, *Journal of Symbolic Logic* **15** (1950) 81–91.

[88] J. Herbrand, *Logical Writings*, (W.D. Goldfarb, Ed.), Harvard, 1971. Translation from: J. Herbrand, *Recherches sur la Théorie de la Demonstration*, Thesis at the University of Paris, 1930.

[89] D. Hilbert, Mathematische Probleme, Vortrag gehalten auf dem internationalen Mathematiker-Kongreß zu Paris, 1900. *Nachr. Ges. Wiss. Göttingen*, math.-phys. Kl., (1900) 253–297. English translation by H.W. Newsom in: *Bulletin of the American Mathematical Society* (1901–1902) 437–479.

[90] J.R. Hindley and J.P. Seldin, (Eds.), *To H.B. Curry: Essays on Combinatory Logic, Lambda Calculus, and Formalism*, Academic, 1980.

[91] J.R. Hindley and J.P. Seldin, *Introduction to Combinators and λ-Calculus*, Cambridge, 1986

[92] C.A.R. Hoare and J.C. Shepherdson, (Eds.), *Mathematical Logic and Programming Languages*, Prentice-Hall, 1985; also in: *Philosophical Transactions of the Royal Society*, Series A, Volume 312, 1984.

[93] S. Hölldobler, *Foundations of Equational Logic Programming*, Lecture Notes in Computer Science **353**, sub-series: Lecture Notes in Artificial Intelligence **X**, Springer, Berlin, 1989.

[94] J.E. Hopcroft and J.D. Ullman, *Introduction to Automata Theory, Languages, and Computation*, Addison-Wesley, 1979.

[95] A. Horn, On sentences which are true of direct unions of algebras, *Journal of Symbolic Logic* **16** (1951) 14–21.

[96] G.P. Huet, The undecidability of unification in third-order logic, *Information and Control* **22** (1973) 257–267.

[97] G.P. Huet, A unification algorithm for typed λ-calculus, *Theoretical Computer Science* **1** (1975) 27–57.

[98] G.P. Huet, *Résolution d'équations dans des Langages d'Ordre* $1, 2, \ldots, \omega$, Thèse de Doctorat d'Etat, Université Paris VII, Paris, 1976.

[99] G.P. Huet, *Solving Equations in Languages of Order* $1, 2, \ldots, \omega$, Translation of the Introduction, Conclusion, and Bibliography of Huet [98] by P. Curtis. Note added to the translation on 1 June 1985 by G.P. Huet.

[100] G.P. Huet, Confluent reductions: abstract properties and applications to term rewriting systems, *Journal of the Association for Computing Machinery* **27**, 4 (1980) 797–821.

[101] G.P. Huet, *Formal Structures for Computation and Deduction*, International Summer School on Logic of Programming and Calculi of Discrete Design, Marktoberdorf, NATO Advanced Study Institutes Programme, 1986.

[102] G.P. Huet and F. Fages, Complete sets of unifiers and matchers in equational theories, *Theoretical Computer Science* **43** 2,3 (1986) 189–200.

[103] G.P. Huet and B. Lang, Proving and applying program transformations expressed with second-order patterns, *Acta Informatica* **11** (1978) 31–55.

[104] G.P. Huet and D.C. Oppen, Equations and rewrite rules: a survey, in: *Formal Languages: Perspectives and Open Problems*, R. Book, (Ed.), Academic, 1980, 349–405.

[105] J.M. Hullot, Canonical forms and unification, *Proceedings of the Fifth Conference on Automated Deduction*, Lecture Notes in Computer Science **87**, Springer, Berlin, 1980, 318–334.

[106] D.C. Jensen and T. Pietrzykowski, Mechanizing ω-order type theory through unification, *Theoretical Computer Science* **3** (1976) 123–171.

[107] P.T. Johnstone, *Topos Theory*, Academic, London, 1977.

[108] J.-P. Jouannaud, and C. Kirchner, Solving equations in abstract algebras: a rule--based survey of unification, Technical report, University of Paris Sud, 1989.

[109] J.-P. Jouannaud and M. Okada, A computational model for executable higher-order algebraic specification languages, *Proceedings of the Sixth Annual IEEE Symposium on Logic in Computer Science*, IEEE Computer Society, Washington, D.C., 1991, 350–361.

[110] C. Kirchner, (Ed.), Unification, Parts I & II, *Journal of Symbolic Computation* (1989) **7**, 3 & 4, and **8**, 1 & 2.

[111] C. Kirchner, (Ed.), *Unification*, Academic, London, 1990.

[112] J. Ketonen, EKL — A mathematically oriented proof checker, *Proceedings of the Seventh Conference on Automated Deduction*, Lecture Notes in Computer Science **170**, Springer, New York, 1984, 65–79.

[113] S.C. Kleene, *Introduction to Metamathematics*, Van Nostrand, Princeton, 1952.

[114] K. Knight, Unification: a multidisciplinary survey, *ACM Computing Surveys* **21** (1989) 93–124.

[115] R.E. Korf, Depth-first iterative-deepening: an optimal admissible tree search, *Artificial Intelligence* **27** (1985) 97-109.

[116] R.A. Kowalski, The early years of logic programming, *Communications of the Association for Computing Machinery* **31** (1988) 38–43.

[117] R. Kowalski, and D. Kuehner, Linear resolution with selection function, *Artificial Intelligence* **2** (1971) 227–260.

[118] S.A. Kripke, Semantical analysis of intuitionistic logic, I, in: *Formal Systems and Recursive Functions*, Proceedings of the Eighth Logic Colloquium, Oxford, J.N. Crossley and M.A.E. Dummett, (Eds.), North-Holland, Amsterdam, 1965, 92–130.

[119] D. Kuehner, Some special purpose resolution systems, in: *Machine Intelligence* **7**, B. Meltzer and D. Michie, (Eds.), Edinburgh, 1972, 117–128.

[120] J. Lambek and P.J. Scott, *Introduction to Higher-Order Categorical Logic*, Cambridge, 1986.

[121] H.R. Lewis and C.H. Papadimitriou, *Elements of the Theory of Computing,* Prentice-Hall, Englewood Cliffs, 1981.

[122] J.W. Lloyd, *Foundations of Logic Programming,* Second edition, Springer, Berlin, 1987.

[123] D.W. Loveland, A linear format for resolution, *Symposium on Automatic Demonstration,* Lecture Notes in Mathematics **125**, Springer, Berlin, 1970, 147–162.

[124] D.W. Loveland, *Automated Theorem Proving: A Logical Basis,* Elsevier North--Holland, New York, 1979.

[125] D.W. Loveland, Automated theorem-proving: a quarter-century review, in: Bledsoe and Loveland (Eds.) [21], 1–45.

[126] D. Luckham, Refinement theorems in resolution theory, *Symposium on Automatic Demonstration,* Lecture Notes in Mathematics **125**, Springer, Berlin, 1970, 163–190.

[127] G.S. Makanin, The problem of the solvability of equations in a free semigroup, *Mat. Sbornik* (New Series) **103** (**145**) (1977) 147–236, 319. English translation in: *Mathematics of the USSR — Sbornik* **32** (1977) 129–198.

[128] J.A. Makowsky, Why Horn formulas matter in computer science: initial structures and generic examples, *Journal of Computer and System Sciences* **34** (1987) 266–292.

[129] P. Martin-Löf, Constructive mathematics and computer programming, in: Hoare and Shepherdson [92], 1985, 167–184.

[130] A. Martelli, and U. Montanari, An efficient unification algorithm. *Association for Computing Machinery Transactions on Programming Languages and Systems* **4** (1982) 258 282.

[131] U. Martin and T. Nipkow, Boolean unification — the story so far, *Journal of Symbolic Computation* **7** (1989) 275–293.

[132] Ju.V. Matiyasevič, Diophantine representation of enumerable predicates, (In Russian), *Izvestija Akademii Nauk SSSR,* Serija Matematika **35** (1971) 3–30. English translation in: *Mathematics of the USSR — Izvestija* **5** (1971) 1–28.

[133] A.R. Meyer, J.C. Mitchell, E. Moggi, and R. Statman, Empty types in polymorphic lambda calculus, in: *Logical Foundations of Functional Programming,* G.P. Huet, (Ed.), Addison-Wesley, 1990, 273–284.

[134] D. Miller, A compact representation of proofs, *Studia Logica* **46** (1987) 345–368.

[135] D. Miller, A logic programming language with lambda-abstraction, function variables, and simple unification, *Journal of Logic and Computation* **1** (1991) 497–536.

[136] D. Miller, E.L. Cohen, and P.B. Andrews, A look at TPS, *Proceedings of the Sixth Conference on Automated Deduction*, Lecture Notes in Computer Science **138**, Springer, New York, 1982, 50–69.

[137] D. Miller and G. Nadathur, Some uses of higher-order logic in computational linguistics, *Proceedings of the 24th Annual Meeting of the Association for Computational Linguistics*, 1986, 247–255.

[138] D. Miller and G. Nadathur, A logic programming approach to manipulating formulas and programs, *Proceedings of the IEEE Fourth Symposium on Logic Programming*, San Francisco, September 1987, 379–388.

[139] D. Miller, G. Nadathur, F. Pfenning, and A. Scedrov, Uniform proofs as a foundation for logic programming, *Annals of Pure and Applied Logic* **51** (1991) 125–157.

[140] J. Minker, *Foundations of Deductive Databases and Logic Programming*, J. Minker, (Ed.), Kaufman, Los Altos, 1987.

[141] J.C. Mitchell, Private communication, 18 April 1989.

[142] J.C. Mitchell, Type Systems for Programming Languages, Report No. STAN-CS-89-1277, Department of Computer Science, Stanford University, July 1989. To appear in: *Handbook of Theoretical Computer Science*, van Leenwen et al., (Eds.), North-Holland.

[143] G. Nadathur and D. Miller, Higher-order Horn clauses, *Journal of the Association for Computing Machinery* **37** (1990) 777–814.

[144] P. Narendran, Some remarks on second order unification, Report, Institute of Programming and Logics, Department of Computer Science, State University of New York at Albany, 1990.

[145] G. Nelson and D.C. Oppen, Fast decision procedures based on congruence closure, *Journal of the Association for Computing Machinery* **27** (1980) 356–364.

[146] T. Nipkow, Higher-order critical pairs, *Sixth Annual IEEE Symposium on Logic in Computer Science*, IEEE Computer Society, Washington, D.C., July 1991, 342–349.

[147] M. O'Donnell, *Equational Logic as a Programming Language*, MIT Press, 1985.

[148] M.S. Paterson and M.N. Wegman, Linear unification, *Journal of Computer and System Sciences* **16** (1978) 158–167.

[149] L.C. Paulson, Natural deduction as higher-order resolution, *Journal of Logic Programming* **3** (1986) 237–258.

[150] L.C. Paulson, *Logic and Computation: Interactive Proof with Cambridge LCF*, Cambridge, 1987.

[151] L.C. Paulson, The foundation of a generic theorem prover, *Journal of Automated Reasoning* **5** (1989) 363–397.

[152] F. Pfenning, Unification and anti-unification in the Calculus of Constructions, *Sixth Annual IEEE Symposium on Logic in Computer Science*, IEEE Computer Society, Washington, D.C., July 1991, 74–85.

[153] T. Pietrzykowski, A complete mechanization of second-order type theory, *Journal of the Association for Computing Machinery* **20** (1973) 333–364.

[154] G.D. Plotkin, Lattice-theoretic properties of subsumption, Memorandum MIP-R-77, University of Edinburgh, 1970.

[155] G.D. Plotkin, A further note on inductive generalization, *Machine Intelligence* **6**, B. Meltzer and D. Michie, (Eds.), Edinburgh, 1971, 101–124.

[156] G.D. Plotkin, Building-in equational theories, in: *Machine Intelligence* **7**, B. Meltzer and D. Michie, (Eds.), Edinburgh, 1972, 73–90.

[157] G.D. Plotkin, λ-Definability and logical relations, Memorandum SAI-RM-4, School of Artificial Intelligence, University of Edinburgh, October 1973.

[158] G.D. Plotkin, Lambda-definability in the full type hierarchy, in: Hindley and Seldin [90], 363–374.

[159] G.D. Plotkin, Message to the TYPES computer mailing list, 29 May 1989.

[160] D. Prawitz, An improved proof procedure, *Theoria* **26** (1960) 102–139.

[161] D. Prawitz, *Natural Deduction: A Proof-Theoretical Study*, Almqvist and Wiksell, Stockholm, 1965.

[162] Z. Qian, Unification of higher-order patterns in linear time and space, Technical Report 5/92, FB 3 Informatik, Universität Bremen, Germany, October 1992.

[163] Z. Qian and K. Wang, Higher-order *E*-unification for arbitrary theories, *Proceedings of the 1992 Joint International Conference and Symposium on Logic Programming*, Washington, D.C., 1992.

[164] F.P. Ramsey, *The Foundations of Mathematics and Other Logical Essays*, Routledge & Kegan Paul, London, 1931.

[165] G.A. Ringwood, SLD: a folk acronym?, *SIGPLAN Notices* **24** (1989) 71–75, Association for Computing Machinery.

[166] J.A. Robinson, A machine-oriented logic based on the resolution principle, *Journal of Association for Computing Machinery* **12**,1 (1965) 23–41.

[167] G. Robinson and L. Wos, Paramodulation and theorem-proving in first-order theories with equality, in: *Machine Intelligence* **4**, B. Meltzer and D. Michie, (Eds.), Edinburgh, 1969, 135–150.

[168] H.E. Rose, *Subrecursion: Functions and Hierarchies*, Oxford, 1984.

[169] D.E. Rydeheard and R.M. Burstall, *Computational Category Theory*, Prentice-Hall, Englewood Cliffs, 1988.

[170] T.J. Schaefer, The complexity of satisfiability problems, *Conference Record of the Tenth Annual ACM Symposium on Theory of Computing*, ACM, New York, 1978, 216–226.

[171] H. Schwichtenberg, Definierbare Funktionen im λ-Kalkül mit Typen, *Archiv für Mathematische Logik und Grundlagenforschung* **17** (1976) 113–114.

[172] D.S. Scott, Identity and existence in intuitionistic logic, in: M.P. Fourman, C.J. Mulvey, and D.S. Scott, (Eds.), *Applications of Sheaves: Proceedings of the Durham Research Symposium on Applications of Sheaf Theory to Logic, Algebra, and Analysis*, Lecture Notes in Mathematics **273**, Springer, Berlin, 1977, 660–696.

[173] J.C. Shepherdson, Negation in logic programming, in: Minker (Ed.) [140], 19–88.

[174] J.H. Siekmann, *Unification and Matching Problems*, Ph.D. Dissertation, Essex University, Memo. CSA-4-78, 1978.

[175] J.H. Siekmann, Universal unification, *Proceedings of the Seventh Conference on Automated Deduction*, Lecture Notes in Computer Science **170**, Springer, New York, 1984, 1–42.

[176] J.H. Siekmann, Unification theory, *Journal of Symbolic Computation* **7** (1989) 207–274.

[177] F.S.K. Silbermann and B. Jayaraman, A domain-theoretic approach to functional and logic programming, Tulane University Technical Report TUTR 91–109, Tulane University, New Orleans, April 1992. To appear in the *Journal of Functional Programming*.

[178] T. Skolem, Logisch-kombinatorische untersuchungen über die erfüllbarkeit oder beweisbarkeit mathematischer Sätze nebst einem Theoreme über dichte Mengen, *Skr. av Videnskapsselskapet i Kristiania, I. Matem.-natur. klasse*, (1920), No. 4.

[179] T. Skolem, Über die mathematische Logik, *Norsk Matematisk Tidsskrift* **10** (1928), 125–142. Translated in van Heijenoort (Ed.) [84], 560–564.

[180] W. Snyder, Higher-order *E*-unification, *Proceedings of the Tenth International Conference on Automated Deduction*, Lecture Notes in Computer Science **449**, Springer, Berlin, 1990, 573–587.

[181] W. Snyder, *A Proof Theory for General Unification*, Birkhäuser, Boston, 1991.

[182] W. Snyder and J. Gallier, Higher-order unification revisited: complete sets of transformations, *Journal of Symbolic Computation* **8** (1989) 101–140.

[183] R. Statman, The typed λ-calculus is not elementary recursive, *Theoretical Computer Science* **9** (1979) 73–81.

[184] R. Statman, On the existence of closed terms in the typed λ-calculus II: transformations of unification problems, *Theoretical Computer Science* **15** (1981) 329–338.

[185] R. Statman, Completeness, invariance, and λ-definability, *Journal of Symbolic Logic* **47**,1 (1982) 17–26.

[186] R. Statman, Equality between functionals revisited, in: L.A. Harrington et al. (Eds.), *Harvey Friedman's Research on the Foundations of Mathematics*, North-Holland, Amsterdam, 1985, 331–338.

[187] R. Statman, Private communication, 25 May 1989.

[188] J. Stern, (Ed.), *Proceedings of the Herbrand Symposium — Logic Colloquium '81*, Studies in Logic and the Foundations of Mathematics **107**, North-Holland, Amsterdam, 1982.

[189] S-Å. Tärnlund, Horn clause computability, BIT **17** (1977) 215–226.

[190] A. Tarski, A lattice-theoretical fixpoint theorem and its applications, *Pacific Journal of Mathematics* **5** (1955) 285–309.

[191] A. Urquhart, Hard examples for resolution, *Journal of the Association for Computing Machinery* **34** (1987) 209–219.

[192] J.S. Vitter and R.A. Simons, New classes for parallel complexity: a study of unification and other complete problems for $\mathcal{P}$, *IEEE Transactions on Computers* **C-35**, 5 (1986) 403–418.

[193] D.H.D. Warren, Higher-order extensions to Prolog: are they needed?, *Machine Intelligence* **10**, J.E. Hayes, D. Michie, and Y.-H. Pao, (Eds.), Halsted, 1982, 441–454.

[194] A.N. Whitehead and B. Russell, *Principia Mathematica*, Cambridge, England, Volume 2, (Second Edition), 1927.

[195] G. Winterstein, Unification in second order logic, *Elektronische Informationsverarbeitung und Kybernetik* **13** (1977) 399–411.

[196] D.A. Wolfram, M.J. Maher, and J-L. Lassez, A unified treatment of resolution strategies for logic programs, *Proceedings of the Second International Logic Programming Conference*, Uppsala, 1984, 263–276.

[197] D. A. Wolfram, Reducing thrashing by Adaptive Backtracking, University of Cambridge Computer Laboratory, Technical Report **112**, August 1987.

[198] D.A. Wolfram, Intractable unifiability problems and backtracking, *Journal of Automated Reasoning* **5** (1989) 37–47.

[199] D.A. Wolfram, Forward checking and intelligent backtracking, *Information Process-ing Letters* **32** (1989) 85–87.

[200] D.A. Wolfram, ACE: the abstract clause engine, System Summary, *Proceedings of the Tenth International Conference on Automated Deduction*, Kaiserslautern, Fed-eral Republic of Germany, 23–27 July 1990, Lecture Notes in Artificial Intelligence **449**, Springer, Berlin, 1990, 679–680.

[201] D.A. Wolfram, Rewriting and equational unification: the higher-order cases, *Proc-eedings of the Fourth International Conference on Rewriting Techniques and Appli-cations, RTA-91*, Lecture Notes in Computer Science **488**, Springer, Berlin, April 1991, 25–36.

[202] L. Wos, S. Winker, and E. Lusk, Semigroups, antiautomorphisms, and involutions: a computer solution to an open problem, *Mathematics of Computation* (1981) 533–545.

[203] M. Zaionc, The set of unifiers in typed λ-calculus as regular expression, *Rewriting Techniques and Applications*, Lecture Notes in Computer Science **202**, Springer, 1985, 430–440.

[204] M. Zaionc, Word operation definable in the typed λ-calculus, *Theoretical Computer Science* **52** (1987) 1–14.

Index